THE PREPPER'S PANTRY

NUTRITIONAL BULK FOOD PREPPING TO MAINTAIN A
HEALTHY DIET AND A STRONG IMMUNE SYSTEM TO
SURVIVE ANY CRISIS

TED RILEY

CONTENTS

A Special Gift to My Readers

Included with your purchase of this book is your free copy of the *Emergency Information Planner*

Follow the link below to receive your copy:
www.tedrileyauthor.com
Or by accessing the QR code:

You can also join our Facebook community **Suburban Prepping with Ted**, or contact me directly via ted@tedrileyauthor.com.

Let thy food be thy medicine and thy medicine be thy food.

— HIPPOCRATES

INTRODUCTION

When you're prepping for an emergency, one of the most important elements to have is food. The general recommendation is to have at least a few days' worth of food on hand at all times, but what good are a few days if you find yourself unable to leave your home for weeks? Especially now, in the wake of the COVID-19 pandemic, it's become clear that sometimes you simply can't leave your home. Maybe the stores are too crowded and supplies are gone. Or maybe you get diagnosed and have to stay at home for at least two weeks. Or what if some other calamity causes you to have to stay put in your home for weeks or even months?

Being prepared in the event of an emergency is one of the best moves you can make. While we all like to think that nothing will happen to us or our families when we're all cozy in our homes, disaster could strike at any time. Whether it's an earthquake that decimates the infrastructure and cuts off the supply routes, the outbreak of war, or even a pandemic that causes a total lockdown, it's essential to have food on hand. But not just any food will do. Having a well-stocked, healthy, nutrient-rich pantry can make the difference between life and death, depending on how long the disaster lasts.

It's easy to say that nothing bad will ever happen to you, and there's a chance that you'll be right. But there's also a chance that you'll be wrong, and you don't want to be left with only your words of regret to eat. Preparing in case of an emergency isn't much different from buying insurance for your car. You have it in case you need it, while hoping that day never comes. However, the day you get into an accident, you'll know that your initial investment was worth it.

Preparing for the worst isn't about paranoia: It's about being prepared so you and your family are kept safe. You want to go to sleep knowing that if anything happens, you've prepared yourself and your family to the best of your ability. Even if you live in a city, being able to bug in, or stay in place until the danger passes, is essential. You'll need food if you want to shelter in place, making no trips out to find food or other resources.

That's what this book is here for. It's hard to know which foods can be safely kept and which ones you'll need to keep yourself healthy. That's why, in this book, you're going to learn about your nutritional requirements and what you can do to meet them, even when you don't have access to grocery stores.

By this stage, you might think that all this sounds great, but why should you believe a word I say? Well, let me introduce myself. My name is Ted Riley, and I've spent my life learning about survival. It all began when I first entered the Boy Scouts, and my love of learning to survive in this crazy, wonderful world has continued since then. I spent more and more time outdoors, learning to live off the land. The outdoors was like my extended home as I'd swim, make my shelters, and even learned to catch and gut fish with my father.

By the age of 10, my family started traveling for work. My father's unique skills meant he was sent all over the world, and while we didn't want for much, we still found ourselves in situations that weren't the safest. I learned about the value of being able to survive in new environments, how to make my presence known, how to assimilate when necessary, and how to make myself disappear.

You might think that what I experienced in countries like Pakistan is nothing like what you'd face in your daily life, but just take a look around you. In 2020, cities and states in America were calling curfews, initially to slow the spread of a deadly virus, and then to prevent violence from riots across the nation. Every country falls apart at some point. Emergencies happen at some point. War and violence are very real parts of the world. Why pretend otherwise?

My early life experiences encouraged me to settle down in Eastern Oklahoma. Here, my family has a homestead, and every day we're one step closer to self-sufficiency. Part of my motivation for this was to enjoy the satisfaction that comes from creating our world and meeting our own needs. However, part of it was influenced by what I saw growing up.

I don't doubt that we'd be able to survive just about anything, and my children have learned about the importance of self-sufficiency and preparedness. It's taken work, but now, I'm able to go to bed each night safe in the knowledge that, no matter what happens, we'll be able to get through it.

Before settling into my home, I dedicated my life to studying survival, both in the wilderness and in urban environments. I knew this was my calling, and now, I have a new one: to share my knowledge with others and ensure that they too can survive and protect themselves and their families. Are you ready to learn about how to keep yourself and your family alive when the world becomes a more dangerous place? Are you ready to build up a contingency plan in case you can't easily access food? By the end of this book, you will have a better idea of how you can keep your family fed and safe no matter what happens. So, let's get started!

1

PREPARING TO BE PREPARED: THE BASICS OF A HEALTHY DIET, AND WHY YOU SHOULD BE FOLLOWING ONE BEFORE DISASTER STRIKES

Bodies are pretty marvelous creations, and despite popular belief, your body doesn't need food just to keep itself alive. Without the right food, your body can't work effectively. You need to understand which foods matter and which ones will not do much more than to keep your belly full. While not feeling hungry is important, if all you eat are things that will not provide you with the nutrients you need, you won't feel much better in the long run.

Your body needs carbohydrates, fats, proteins, and fiber to function properly. Beyond that, it requires trace amounts of several vitamins and minerals. These micronutrients are used to keep your body functioning properly. Your cells need them to complete their intended functions so your body stays alive.

You're probably healthy now, but do you know how to keep yourself healthy when supplies are limited? What are you going to do if you can't get hold of fresh, healthy produce? When so much of the long-life food available isn't very healthy or conducive to keeping you alive, would you know how to keep yourself and your family feeling well?

Understanding the ins and outs of a healthy diet is crucial if you want to understand how to meet those requirements in desperate times as well as in times of stability. Even though you might be a master at making organic, healthy, balanced meals now, you might not manage so well if all you have are some canned goods and you don't know what to focus on. Now, you're in luck because pre-packaged food is required to be labeled with its nutritional facts. However, if you don't know what your body needs, can you be sure you're meeting its requirements?

The average adult needs somewhere between 2,000 and 2,500 calories each day, depending on how physical they are. Beyond just caloric intake, they must also take in the right macronutrient ratios. You can't just eat 2,500 calories' worth of sugar and expect your body to function properly. Likewise, 2,500 calories' worth of fat or protein won't keep you full and energized. You need to balance them out just right.

Macronutrients

Macronutrients are the parts of food that we commonly think of as the major food components: carbs, proteins, fats, and fiber. These are important in different ratios to ensure that your body works well.

Carbohydrates

Most people hear the word "carbs" and think of sugar. Sugars are often considered unhealthy, but that's a bit of a misconception. While you should limit added sugars and processed carbohydrates, natural sugars are a great way to get a quick energy boost and help you feel ready to take on anything.

Carbohydrates serve as your body's major source of energy. They are the sugars, starches, and fiber you consume when you eat fruits, vegetables, grains, or dairy products. Typically, we categorize these as either simple or complex carbohydrates, depending on how they are broken down by the body. Some diets may recommend that you cut them out entirely, but they are essential to a long-term healthy diet. Your body needs them to continue moving and functioning at the optimum level.

Adults are typically recommended to consume roughly 45–65% of their daily calories through carbohydrates, preferably complex. However, every person is going to have different needs. Let's say you need to eat at least 2,000 calories per day. 1 gram of carbohydrates is roughly 4 calories, so if you need 2,000 calories, eat somewhere between 225 and 325 grams of carbs each day. The National Institutes of Health (NIH) recommends at least 135 grams per day. Diabetics are recommended to limit their intake to only 200 grams, while pregnant women are told not to eat less than 175 grams. We mustn't forget the kids either: Children have different dietary requirements, depending on their ages and activity levels.

The carbs you consume are essential for your nervous system and muscles. They allow your body to keep its activity level normal and regulated without needing to break down muscle or fat. Because they're quick to metabolize, they're easy for the body to use for quick energy.

Not all carbs are good carbs, however, and you'll need to take into consideration whether they're simple or complex. The difference between the two is how quickly your body can break down and absorb the sugars within them.

Simple carbs are those that contain just one or two sugars, such as fructose and galactose, which you can get in fruits and milk products, respectively. These single sugars are known as monosaccharides. Carbs with two sugars within them are known as disaccharides. These are sugars such as sucrose, lactose, or maltose, which are found in table sugar, dairy, and beer respectively.

These sugars all come with other nutritional values, such as fiber, vitamins, and minerals. For example, an apple might be loaded with sugar, but it also comes with vitamins, minerals, and fiber that make them healthier. Refined sugars are little more than the empty calories that are typically associated with weight gain, coming from sources such as:

- Candy bars
- Potato chips
- Soda

- Table sugar
- White bread

Complex carbs are those with three or more sugars, and are typically thought of as starchy foods. Common ones include:

- Beans
- Corn
- Lentils
- Parsnips
- Peanuts
- Peas
- Potatoes
- Whole-grain bread, cereals, and pasta

While all carbs are digested quickly and easily, simple carbs are digested much quicker. They provide a quick burst of energy, but your body also quickly burns through them. Complex carbohydrates take much longer to break down, which means instead of getting the quick sugar high followed by a crash, you'll get sustained energy. This is what you should aim for when looking at what foods to keep in your pantry.

Proteins

Proteins are essential in creating muscle mass in the body, and they are primarily found in animal products, although there are some great vegetarian sources. A single gram of protein is roughly 4 calories, and your body's weight is ideally about 15% protein.

Proteins are made up of amino acids, built from carbon, nitrogen, hydrogen, sulfur, or oxygen. They are consumed and broken down to create more muscle mass. The more muscle mass you have, the faster your metabolism.

Protein also keeps you feeling fuller longer. According to a 2014 study published in *Nutrition*, when people consume high-protein yogurt as a snack, they feel fuller longer than if they had high-fat crackers. The high-protein snack also caused satiety that made them less hungry at dinner. Beyond just providing satiety, protein is also known to improve the immune system, which we'll be addressing in depth in the next chapter. It provides essential amino acids that will help your body's immune system to fend off foreign bodies, while also allowing for the rebuilding and healing of cells.

Protein should make up between 10% and 35% of your diet each day, depending on your activity level, weight, age, and sex. While it's easy for people to get protein throughout their day, most people get it from fatty sources. Lean proteins should be emphasized. There are several important sources of protein that you can enjoy, with many of them also vegetarian. Foods that are protein rich include:

- Beans
- Eggs
- Meat
- Nuts and seeds
- Peas
- Poultry
- Soy products

It's recommended that you consume between 20 and 30 grams of protein per meal. That is the equivalent of 3–4 ounces of meat or 2.5 egg whites. Most women don't get enough protein in the mornings, which can be problematic for both hormone regulation and boosting metabolism.

Fats

Fats get a poor reputation in the dieting world, but they're incredibly important. Fats serve an important purpose: They act as storage for energy. Fat is significantly more calorie-dense than proteins and carbs, with 9 calories per gram. Fats also aid in vitamin absorption, keeping skin and hair healthy, adding insulation to the body, and helping to protect organs.

However, fat must be consumed in moderation. It is recommended that you get 20–30% of your calories from healthy fat sources each day, coming in at around 44–78 grams daily. As essential as it is, too much fat can quickly lead to increased levels of fat in the body as well, which can be detrimental to your health. You can't just skip the fat entirely, and often, low-fat options are unhealthy for you because they're filled up with sugar to make them taste better. But you also need to make sure that you eat the right kinds of fats.

Fats come in several varieties, with some being beneficial and others harmful. Saturated and trans fats are typically regarded as unhealthy, while unsaturated fats are healthier for you.

- **Saturated fats:** Saturated fats are those that are saturated with hydrogen molecules and typically, they come from animal sources. They are usually solid at room temperature, like cheese, butter, and certain oils, such as coconut oil. High levels of saturated fats are linked to higher cholesterol levels, which can put you at an increased risk for cardiovascular disease. They also are high in calories. You should get only 5–6% of your calories (roughly 13 grams) per day from saturated fats, according to the American Heart Association.

- **Monounsaturated fats:** Monounsaturated fats are those that are liquid at room temperature. They are beneficial to the human body, aiding in improving cholesterol levels and protecting the heart. They also may aid in regulating blood sugar and insulin levels, according to the Mayo Clinic. You usually find these in avocados and olives and their associated oils, such as extra virgin olive oil. Despite being healthier, it's important to recognize that you still need to be mindful of how many calories you take in from healthy sources.

- **Polyunsaturated fats:** Polyunsaturated fats are also liquid at room temperature. They've got more than one carbon bond in their fat molecules, which is how they get their name. They are commonly found from plant food sources like soybeans, sunflower seeds, walnuts, and flaxseeds. They are also found in fatty fish like herring, trout, tuna, and salmon. These forms of fat decrease the risk of cardiovascular disease while also aiding in cell development and maintenance. They also provide essential fatty acids, including omega-6 and omega-3 fatty acids.

- Omega-3s allow for lowered blood pressure and act as anti-inflammatories.
- Omega-6 fatty acids also help the body, improving bone health, benefitting the reproductive system, and promoting healthy skin and hair. However, in excess, omega-6 fatty acids can be inflammatory.
- **Trans fats (trans fatty acids):** These fats occur naturally, especially in meat or dairy, but typically are only present in small amounts. They are most often found in processed foods, baked goods, refrigerated dough, coffee creamer, fast food, and margarine. They are linked to heart disease and weight gain, and in 2013, they were declared by the FDA to no longer be safe. Artificial trans fats are banned in the United States. Don't bother stocking up on too many of these.

Fiber

Fiber is an essential macronutrient, but not for the same reason as the others. The other three—carbohydrates, protein, and fats—are broken down to provide energy for the body. However, fiber cannot be digested to provide energy. Rather, it is used to aid the digestive system, and you get health benefits from it.

Fiber prevents us from becoming constipated, and the US as a whole misses out on the right levels of fiber needed for health benefits. The average American adult consumes only 15 grams of fiber, while it's recommended that you should consume significantly more. Women are recommended to consume at least 25 grams up until the age of 50, at which point the recommendation drops to 21 grams. For men, 38 grams is recommended, and at age 50, that recommendation goes down to 30 grams.

Fiber is comprised of roughage: the fibers found in fruits and vegetables that you can't digest. You might think that if they can't be digested, why bother eating them at all? The answer is simple: because you want to move food along in your digestive system. If you want to get the waste out of your body, you need to have something that can move that waste through once you've digested enough of the food. That comes from the fiber. As you bulk your diet up with fiber, the waste can be excreted quicker.

It's also essential if you want to keep yourself feeling full. Fiber feels heavy in the stomach, and because of that, it can help you feel full and lose weight, as it cuts out the need to snack. Beyond just helping to keep you regular, fiber protects from a wide range of chronic diseases, such as heart disease, cancer, and type 2 diabetes.

It is essential for feeding the healthy Microbiome in the intestines. In many heart foods this is called probiotics. A healthy Microbiome is responsible for maintaining a healthy immune system.

You can bulk up your food with added dietary fiber from many easy sources. For example, you can expect to get plenty of fiber from grains, fruits, and vegetables.

Micronutrients

Your body also needs vitamins and minerals to stay healthy. We commonly refer to these as micronutrients, and while they're needed in smaller quantities than the macronutrients, they're still essential to your health and wellbeing. Your body cannot create these micronutrients itself, so it must get them from other sources.

Vitamins vs. Minerals

Vitamins are crucial for your body's functions, from producing energy to regulating the immune system or blood clotting. Minerals are used for your body to grow, balance fluids, and keep your bones dense. The vitamins that you consume are organic compounds that plants and animals make, which may be altered or broken down by heat, acid, or air. You absorb these vitamins and minerals as you eat, allowing your body to function.

Minerals

Your body requires a combination of macrominerals and trace minerals to function properly. Macrominerals are required in higher quantities, while trace minerals are required in smaller quantities.

Macrominerals

- **Calcium:** This allows for the creation of bones and teeth, while also aiding in muscle function and the contraction of blood vessels.
- **Chloride:** Typically found in table salt with sodium. It aids in fluid balance and helps to create digestive juices.
- **Magnesium:** This aids in over 300 enzyme reactions, and also helps to regulate blood pressure.
- **Phosphorus:** This aids in the formation of bones and cell membranes.
- **Potassium:** This is an electrolyte that helps balance and regulate fluids in cells, nerve transmission, and muscle function.
- **Sodium:** This is an essential electrolyte that

allows for fluid balance and controls blood pressure.

- **Sulfur:** Every living tissue requires sulfur, and it's a part of the amino acids methionine and cysteine.

Trace minerals

Your body needs fewer trace minerals, but they're still essential for many purposes.

- **Copper:** This is necessary for connective tissue formation and helps your nervous system and brain to function properly.
- **Fluoride:** This helps bone and teeth to develop.
- **Iodine:** This aids in thyroid functionality and regulation.
- **Iron:** Iron allows for oxygen to be processed by muscles and aids in creating certain hormones.
- **Manganese:** Manganese works in aiding carbohydrate, cholesterol, and amino acid metabolism.
- **Selenium:** This helps with thyroid health, while also being essential for reproduction and as an antioxidant.
- **Zinc:** This is necessary to help with healing, immune function, and normal growth.

Vitamins

Vitamins are essential and come from many natural sources. You'll find them in many healthy foods. Some animals can produce certain vitamins, while others need to get them from food sources. They are organic compounds that will help keep you healthy. Some are fat-soluble and others are water-soluble. Your body can store fat-soluble vitamins for future use, but it can't store water-soluble vitamins for very long.

Vitamin A

Vitamin A is also known as retinol. It's fat-soluble and essential for your eyes. Without enough vitamin A, you may suffer from night blindness. You can get it from foods such as:

- Apricots
- Broccoli
- Butter
- Cantaloupe
- Carrots
- Collard greens
- Eggs
- Kale
- Liver
- Milk
- Pumpkin
- Spinach
- Sweet potatoes

Vitamin B

Vitamin B is water-soluble and comes in several forms with different names:

- **Vitamin B1 (Thiamine):** This vitamin produces enzymes to break down blood sugar. You can get it from foods like yeast, pork, sunflower seeds, brown rice, asparagus, cauliflower, and potatoes.

- **Vitamin B2 (Riboflavin):** It's necessary to help the body develop cells and aid metabolism. You can find this vitamin in foods like asparagus, bananas, fish, yogurt, meat, eggs, and chard.
- **Vitamin B3 (Niacin):** Also known as niacinamide. Your body requires it so cells can grow and work. You can get it from eggs, salmon, milk, beef, tuna, leafy greens, broccoli, and carrots.
- **Vitamin B5 (Pantothenic Acid):** It helps with creating energy and maintaining hormone regulation. It's found in meat, broccoli, avocado, whole grains, and yogurt.
- **Vitamin B6 (Pyridoxine):** It is necessary for the creation of red blood cells and can be found in chickpeas, liver, bananas, and nuts.
- **Vitamin B7 (Biotin):** It is used to metabolize proteins, fats, and carbs. It also helps to produce keratin, which your body needs to create hair, nails, and skin.
- **Vitamin B9 (Folic Acid):** It is essential to make DNA and RNA. It's especially important for women of child-bearing age, as early deficiencies can affect fetal nervous systems

before women even know they're pregnant. It's recommended to be supplemented for this reason, even if you're not pregnant. It's commonly found in leafy greens, liver, peas, legumes, fruits, and many fortified grain products. If you're a woman, or live with a woman who may become pregnant, keeping foods fortified in folic acid is essential.

- **Vitamin B12 (Cyanocobalamin):** It's necessary in order to create a healthy nervous system. It can be found in fish, shellfish, meat, poultry, milk, and eggs.

Vitamin C

Vitamin C, or ascorbic acid, is a water-soluble vitamin that our bodies use to help with wound healing and bone formation. It aids in producing collagen, and builds strong and healthy blood vessels, while also boosting the immune system. It plays a vital role in the absorption of iron, and is also antioxidant in nature. Without it, you can develop scurvy, which causes problems with healing and tissue growth, and can result in the loss of teeth. You can find vitamin C in most fruits and vegetables, but they have to be eaten raw, as cooking destroys it.

Vitamin D

Vitamin D is known as ergocalciferol or cholecalciferol. It's a fat-soluble vitamin that your body needs to help it develop bones. Without it, you may suffer from softening bones or rickets. You can get vitamin D through sun exposure which triggers your body to produce it. Alternatively, you can get it from fatty fish, beef liver, eggs, or mushrooms.

Vitamin E

Vitamin E is referred to as tocopherol, and it is also fat-soluble. It is an antioxidant, reducing and preventing oxidative stress. It can be found in kiwis, wheat germ, eggs, almonds, nuts, vegetable oils, and leafy greens.

Vitamin K

Also called phylloquinone, vitamin K is fat-soluble and is crucial for blood clotting. Without it, you may bleed too much. It can be found in leafy greens, pumpkin, figs, parsley, and natto.

Choline

Choline is a bit of a special case. Although not classified as a vitamin, it is a nutrient that your body needs. Your body can produce some choline, but you also have to consume it in order to stay healthy. This essential nutrient is organic and water-soluble, but is neither a vitamin nor a mineral. It is commonly grouped with the B vitamins because it is similar in what it does; it's necessary for liver function, metabolism, muscle movements, brain development, and regulating the nervous system. It's essential for optimal health. You can get it from liver, eggs, cod, salmon, broccoli, and cauliflower. Eggs are an excellent source, supplying roughly 25% of your daily requirement.

Recommended Daily Intake

NUTRIENT	INFANTS 12 MONTHS AND UNDER	CHILDREN 1-3 YEARS OLD	ADULTS AND CHILDREN AGED 4 AND OLDER	PREGNANT AND LACTATING WOMEN
BIOTIN	6 MCG	8 MCG	30 MCG	35 MCG
CALCIUM	260 MG	700 MG	1,300 MG	1,300 MG
CHLORIDE	570 MG	1,500 MG	2,300 MG	2,300 MG
CHOLINE	150 MG	200 MG	550 MG	550 MG
CHROMIUM	5.5 MCG	11 MCG	35 MCG	45 MCG
COPPER	0.2 MG	0.3 MG	0.9 MG	1.3 MG
FOLATE	80 MCG	150 MCG	400 MCG	600 MCG
IODINE	130 MCG	90 MCG	150 MCG	290 MCG
IRON	11 MG	7 MG	18 MG	27 MG

NUTRIENT	INFANTS 12 MONTHS AND UNDER	CHILDREN 1-3 YEARS OLD	ADULTS AND CHILDREN AGED 4 AND OLDER	PREGNANT AND LACTATING WOMEN
MAGNESIUM	75 MG	80 MG	420 MG	400 MG
MANGANESE	0.6 MG	1.2 MG	2.3 MG	2.6 MG
MOLYBDENUM	3 MCG	17 MCG	45 MCG	50 MCG
NIACIN	4 MG	6 MG	16 MG	18 MG
PANTOTHENIC ACID	1.8 MG	2 MG	5 MG	7 MG
PHOSPHORUS	275 MG	460 MG	1,250 MG	1,250 MG
POTASSIUM	700 MG	3,000 MG	4,700 MG	5,100 MG
RIBOFLAVIN	0.4 MG	0.5 MG	1.3 MG	1.6 MG
SELENIUM	20 MCG	20 MCG	55 MCG	70 MCG

NUTRIENT	INFANTS 12 MONTHS AND UNDER	CHILDREN 1-3 YEARS OLD	ADULTS AND CHILDREN AGED 4 AND OLDER	PREGNANT AND LACTATING WOMEN
THIAMINE	0.3 MG	0.5 MG	1.2 MG	1.4 MG
VITAMIN A	500 MCG	300 MCG	900 MCG	1,300 MCG
VITAMIN B6	0.3 MG	0.5 MG	1.7 MG	2 MG
VITAMIN B12	0.5 MCG	0.9 MCG	2.4 MCG	2.8 MCG
VITAMIN C	50 MG	15 MG	90 MG	120 MG
VITAMIN D	10 MCG	15 MCG	20 MCG	15 MCG
VITAMIN E	5 MG	6 MG	15 MG	19 MG
VITAMIN K	2.5 MCG	30 MCG	120 MCG	90 MCG
ZINC	3 MG	3 MG	11 MG	13 MG

Chapter Summary

In this chapter, we went over the importance of your diet to your immune system, while also emphasizing what your body will need so you can prep accordingly.

- The average adult will need between 2,000 and 2,500 calories each day.
- The main macronutrients your body needs are carbohydrates, proteins, and fats, which should all come from healthy sources.
- Your body needs fiber to regulate itself and help with digestion.
- There are several micronutrients that your body needs; the vitamins and minerals are taken in from your food.

2

FIGHTING FIT: EAT FOR IMMUNE HEALTH TO PROTECT YOU FROM HEALTH DISASTERS

You only have one body, and you need to protect it to the best of your ability. You know that there are certain things you need to do in order to keep yourself safe. You wouldn't, for example, jump off a cliff and expect to come out of it unscathed. You understand that jumping from some sort of height would likely cause you some sort of harm. You need to make sure that you're safe. What you rarely think of, however, is that you also need to make sure that you're healthy internally as well.

Your body is built to survive. It's able to overcome most challenges that come its way. If you eat something that is not good for you, you're probably in for a few bad days, but your body will recover. If you get sick, you'll usually be able to kick it, so long as it isn't too bad. If you get a cut, your immune system is likely to be strong enough to fend off infection. But your immune system is only good enough to do so if you set it up properly. Support your body if you want that immune system in tip-top shape.

THE HUMAN SECURITY SYSTEM: THE IMMUNE SYSTEM

Your immune system is composed of organs, cells, and chemicals that work in harmony to fight off infection. They all work together to kill microbes that could pose a risk to your body. From bacteria to viruses and foreign bodies, your body uses the immune system to treat problems. Understanding how your immune system works will help you understand what you need to do to support it. Together, the components of your immune system function as a security system to fend off invaders.

White Blood Cells

At the heart of your immune system are the white blood cells. These are created in your bone marrow and are found within the lymphatic system. The white blood cells are transmitted through your body, traveling in the blood and throughout the tissue. They identify microbes that have entered your body to attack them. When your body detects microbes, the white blood cells then send lymphocytes, among other cells, to the source to destroy the microbes and prevent an all-out infection. Without this initial response, your body wouldn't be able to fend off bacteria, viruses, fungi, or parasites, and they'd be able to spread until they took over your body.

Antibodies

Antibodies are used to fend off microbes or any toxins that may be produced by them. Your antibodies will recognize antigens on microbes. Antigens are essentially signatures on the outside of the microbe that allow for antibodies to recognize their presence. Then, upon matching to the antigens, they can identify the toxins or microbes as a foreign body. At that point, they are marked for destruction, and the rest of the immune system tackles it.

Lymphatic System

The lymphatic system is a system of several delicate tubes that spread throughout the body. These serve many important roles, such as managing the fluid levels in your body and responding to bacteria, cell products, or cancer cells. The lymphatic system also works to absorb some fats from the intestines. It is comprised of several essential parts, including:

- Lymph nodes (sometimes called glands), which trap microbes. You may notice them swelling as they collect microbes in the event of infection.
- Lymph vessels, which are the tubes that allow lymph to flow throughout your body. Lymph is a clear liquid that washes through your tissue and is filled with white blood cells.
- White blood cells (also known as lymphocytes).

Complement System

The complement system is an amalgamation of the proteins that work to support the work of the antibodies.

Thymus

The thymus is an important gland in your chest, found between your lungs and right behind your breastbone. It's an essential part of the lymphatic system, and makes T lymphocytes, sometimes called T cells. These T cells can fend off infection.

Spleen

The spleen is an organ that filters your blood. In filtering it, it's able to destroy old, damaged blood cells and also removes microbes that may have been trapped by the immune system. It can also create antibodies and lymphocytes to aid in the support of the immune system.

Bone Marrow

Bone marrow is found within your bones and creates blood. It produces red and white blood cells, while also creating necessary platelets, which are used to clot the blood.

Skin

Your skin is the largest organ in your body, and serves an essential purpose: It creates a waterproof barrier that also secretes an oil used to kill bacteria. Most microbes cannot penetrate the skin if there is not a wound or other opening for them to enter.

Lungs

As you breathe in and out, you pull air into your lungs. That air is filled with many microbes from around you. These microbes would have easy access to the body if the lungs didn't have some protection. They've got mucus within them to trap any foreign particles, and within your lungs you also have cilia, small hairs that work to force the mucus out of your body as you cough.

Digestive Tract

The digestive tract is also lined with mucus. This mucus contains antibodies that protect you. In addition, the acid in your stomach is fatal for most microbes.

Other Important Defense Mechanisms

Your immune system isn't the only line of defense you have against microbes. While it's an essential part, your immune system is more like the security guard to catch anything that slipped through the gate. The other important defense mechanisms are the deterrents to keep the microbes from entering.

Other Common Defenses

Your body also uses other defenses to prevent bacteria from building up. Your bodily fluids are typically designed to protect you. Skin oil, saliva, and tears work to flush out bacteria and are antibacterial to lessen the risk of infection. You flush your urinary tract and bowels regularly, which also helps to force any microbes out.

Fever is also a common defense and immune system response. When you get ill, you might notice that you end up with a fever. This is because your body is trying to kill off the microbes while also creating conditions that are more favorable for your body to repair any damage.

LIFESTYLE FACTORS FOR IMMUNE HEALTH

Now that you know how amazing the body is and what important functions it performs, you need to understand what lifestyle choices benefit and damage your high-performing body. If you want a healthy immune system, one of the easiest ways that you can achieve it is by ensuring that you keep up with your health. Enjoying a healthy body helps to support your immune system. When you've got a healthy body, there's a good chance that most immune responses will not be a big deal. There are other factors that you can remember to keep your immune response healthy as well. By ensuring that you live a healthy lifestyle, you're much more likely to keep a healthy immune system.

Don't Smoke

One of the most frequently stressed rules for keeping a healthy immune system is to remember that smoking is awful for your health. As you smoke, you damage your lungs, which, as we discussed, is one of the more important barriers you have between your body and microbes.

Exercise Regularly

Exercising helps to keep other parts of your body, like your heart and lungs, healthy. It also keeps the blood pumping throughout your body.

Eat Healthily

A healthy diet can provide you with everything you'd need to support your immune system. The vitamins and minerals you consume will help to prepare all essential parts of your immune system so you're ready to go when the need arises.

Maintain a Healthy Weight

Keeping your weight healthy means that your body is healthier overall. You'll have a lower risk of stroke, heart disease, and diabetes, amongst other dangerous conditions. Studies have also shown that too much fat can trigger your immune system to behave erratically.

Drink Alcohol in Moderation

When you drink, you impair your body's immune system as well, except the damage lasts far longer than the intoxication does. You risk harming the lungs, for example. Your gut bacteria can be killed off as well, which may also boost the risk of infection. Alcohol can be inflammatory in the gut. Because your body has to prioritize processing what you drank, it can't focus on the immune system. And, because it causes your sleep to worsen, you weaken your immune system even more. If you're going to drink, make sure that you're drinking in moderation. Binge drinking, in particular, can be an immense problem, and research has shown that if you regularly drink over 14 drinks per week, or over five or six drinks in one sitting, you will directly suppress your immune system.

Quality Sleep

Your body uses sleep as a chance to take care of itself. It is essentially the maintenance period that allows the body to put more effort into the immune system. So when you're sick, you're usually sleepier and sleep for longer. During sleep, energy can be directed directly to the immune system. As you rest, there is a boost in cytokines, which are associated with the immune system and inflammation. Even when you're not sick or hurt, the cytokine production goes up at night, likely to boost adaptive immunity so you can trigger your immune system to remember antigens in the future. By making sure you get quality sleep, you can ensure that your body's immune system is in top condition.

Good Hygiene

Cleanliness is essential if you want to have good hygiene, but too much cleanliness can be problematic as well. You're constantly in contact with millions of germs, but by practicing good personal hygiene, you can protect yourself. Just washing your hands regularly is a great way to protect yourself from infections. You don't need your home to be spotless and bacteria-free. Some bacteria are not very harmful at all and can also keep your immune system functioning normally.

Mindfulness for Stress Reduction

Stress is harmful to your immune system, as precious resources are redistributed elsewhere. When you're stressed, the level of lymphocytes is decreased, which then puts you at an increased risk for illnesses. This is because stress causes cortisol to build in your body, and too much cortisol causes more inflammation. This is where mindfulness comes into play. Mindfulness helps to reduce your stress, which drops your cortisol levels and allows your body to be healthier.

Micronutrients and Immune Health

We've already gone over several of the most essential micronutrients your body needs to function. Many of those are directly related to the immune system, including the following:

- **Carotenoids:** Carotenoids boost the immune system because they can be converted into Vitamin A.
- **Copper:** Copper is important in the creation of red blood cells and helps the immune system to maintain its nerve cells.
- **Folic Acid:** Folic acid encourages cell growth and development to heal wounds and tissue. It also boosts the production of antibodies.
- **Iron:** Iron allows for the production of white blood cells and slows the production of bacteria.
- **Probiotics:** Your entire gut system is lined with a system of bacteria and other microbiota that influence how your body works. Probiotics work to suppress bad bacteria while boosting good bacteria. They also have been shown to create natural antibodies and boost immune cells.
- **Selenium:** Selenium reduces inflammation and is powerful in protecting against respiratory infections.
- **Vitamin A:** Vitamin A regulates antibacterial and anti-inflammatory immune responses.
- **Vitamin B6:** Vitamin B6 is used for the production of white blood cells and T cells. It also allows for the creation of the protein

interleukin-2, which directs white blood cells.

- **Vitamin C:** Vitamin C possesses antibacterial and anti-inflammatory properties and stimulates the production of antibodies and white blood cells.
- **Vitamin E:** Vitamin E is found in higher concentrations in immune cells and regulates the number of natural killer cells. Deficiency impairs the immune system.
- **Zinc:** Zinc reduces inflammation, while also serving as an antiviral. It has been shown to boost natural killer cell activity.

Whole Foods to Boost Your Immune System

If you want to boost your immune system, one of the best all-natural methods of doing so is to include as many healthy foods as you can in your daily diet. Consider the following as staples if you can get your hands on them:

- **Almonds:** Almonds and other nuts are full of vitamin E, which is a fat-soluble vitamin. With just ½ cup of almonds, you can get your total daily quota of vitamin E.
- **Bell Peppers:** Bell peppers, especially red ones, have a massive amount of vitamin C and beta

carotene. They are one of the best sources of vitamin C.

- **Broccoli:** Broccoli is loaded with vitamins A, C, and E, plus it's filled with fiber. However, it loses many of its benefits when it's cooked: Eat it raw or lightly steam it.
- **Garlic:** Garlic not only tastes great, but it is also known to have a high concentration of allicin within it. This sulfur-containing compound is believed to aid in fighting off infections, and garlic was commonly turned to as an antibiotic in ancient civilizations.
- **Ginger:** Like garlic, many have turned to ginger to help reduce illness. It decreases inflammation in the body.
- **Grapefruit:** Grapefruit, like most citrus fruits, is high in vitamin C. Your body cannot store Vitamin C on its own, so you need to get enough of it each day to remain healthy.
- **Green Tea:** Green and black teas are both loaded with flavonoids, which are antioxidants. They are also packed with L-theanine, an amino acid that is believed to help produce T cells.
- **Kiwis:** Kiwis are full of essential elements, including folate, potassium, vitamin K, and vitamin C. These nutrients help to create white

blood cells and to support the rest of your body's functions.

- **Papaya:** Papaya is full of vitamin C, with double the daily recommended value in just one medium-sized fruit. It also contains papain, which has anti-inflammatory effects, and is rich in folate.
- **Poultry:** Poultry is a fantastic choice if you want to boost the immune system. Chicken and turkey are full of vitamin B6. And, when you use the bones to create a bone broth, you'll also get beneficial gelatin and other nutrients that will boost your health.
- **Shellfish:** Shellfish is rich in zinc, especially if you choose mussels, lobster, crab, or oysters. However, make sure you don't eat too much: More than the recommended amount of zinc can inhibit your immune system.
- **Spinach:** Spinach is high in vitamin C, beta carotene, and many antioxidants. It is incredibly healthy if you eat it raw, or with as little cooking as possible.
- **Sunflower Seeds:** Sunflower seeds are loaded with phosphorus, magnesium, and vitamins B6 and E. They are also rich in selenium, with one ounce of sunflower seeds containing nearly half of your recommended daily allowance.

- **Turmeric:** Turmeric is a widely used anti-inflammatory that is rich in curcumin. Curcumin is believed to be an immune booster and has some antiviral properties.
- **Yogurt:** Yogurt, especially Greek yogurt, is full of good bacteria that help your digestive system. Look for "live and active cultures" on the label, and choose plain varieties over other kinds. You can sweeten it with a bit of honey and fruit.

We rarely think much about what we do day to day and how those actions may affect our health. However, everything that you do in your life, from how much you sleep to what you choose to eat, will affect your health. Your immune system is your first line of defense against any harm or illness that may come your way. Living a healthy lifestyle is the best way to keep yourself healthy. This means emphasizing healthier foods, sleeping well, and exercising regularly.

Chapter Summary

In this chapter, we discussed the importance of lifestyle on your immune system. Some of the most important points include:

- The immune system protects the body from

illnesses, and is therefore essential for ensuring that, in an emergency, you are healthy.

- Diet and lifestyle both directly influence the immune system.
- Foods rich in certain vitamins and minerals are essential for your immune system's health.

3

AN ESSENTIAL GROCERY CART LIST FOR HEALTHY SURVIVAL

Grocery stores only keep roughly three days' worth of food on hand. One thing that COVID-19 showed was that as soon as some shelves look a little empty, the panic shopping begins. People are terrified of not having enough food on hand because, without the right amount of food, how are they supposed to feed and provide for their families? How are they going to ensure that their children have enough food to eat?

The supply chain is not very efficient at dealing with delays. You don't want to be caught with empty shelves when an emergency happens, and you don't want to have to beat the rush as everyone tries to get to the store at the same time. In the event of an emergency, most people will only have a few days' worth of food stocked and they will have no other choice than to flock to the stores.

With the basics under your belt and an understanding of what your body needs, you can start planning the essentials for your food stores. Because there are so many foods that you'll want to keep stocked up, you may need to do multiple shopping trips to get everything in the right quantities. One of the most important elements of putting together a prepper's pantry is understanding that you will not go out on one big trip and get everything you need all at once. There are a couple of reasons for this, which we will discuss later in the chapter.

As you read over this chapter and the next, you may realize that some items on the second list make more sense to stock up on sooner rather than later. Customize how you choose to shop based on what you have available to you according to your location, needs, and circumstances.

This chapter will introduce you to several important aspects of stockpiling. It will include the importance of reducing the costs of your purchases, while also exploring the idea of setting up a garden for yourself to ensure that you've got plenty of food on hand. Even if you have limited space available, there are methods you can use to garden within your space constraints.

We will address the essential FEMA recommendations for disaster preparedness, as well as go over a list of the best foods that you should prioritize in your stockpile. By the time you've finished reading, you will have a pretty good idea of what you should start stocking up on and why.

Reducing Costs with Bulk Buying

Shopping to stock your home is not likely to be cheap, especially if you have a large family to take care of. However, by shopping well, you should be able to keep the prices down. When you buy in bulk, you're able to shave down some costs. This is because bulk quantities of food use less packaging. You also get a discount for bulk quantities. Even if your family doesn't need things in bulk, you can still break them down and package them in smaller rations. For example, imagine you buy a big, 20-pound bag of rice. You will be able to break it down into much smaller increments, or you could keep it in one large bucket. For storing food, you have a lot of options.

Consider some of these tips for reducing the cost as you begin your stockpile:

Check Flyers Regularly

Stores usually change their prices weekly, so you're likely to see fresh foods that you may want to buy in bulk come on sale in different time frames. For example, maybe you are stockpiling chicken. That chicken may be $2.99 per pound this week or $1.59 per pound next week. If you were only trying to buy enough for your family of four to eat a couple of meals in a week, you might not think much of buying 3 pounds for $8.97 today instead of waiting two days and making an extra trip to buy it for just $4.77 when it goes on sale again. The additional $4.20 may not be worth the effort and cost of gas to go to the store again.

However, when you run that math again with larger quantities, such as if you wanted to stockpile 50 pounds of meat, the difference is much more pronounced: at $2.99/lb, you're going to spend $149.50 on that meat. However, if you were to go back a few days later for the cheaper price, you'd spend just $79.50. The difference is $70. At that price point, it's probably worth making a repeat shopping trip. Depending on how close you are to the store, you could ride a bicycle and take a cold bag, and squeeze in some more exercise on the way.

Pay attention to the ads and flyers as you shop and plan your trips. If possible, you could even shop on the day before your local store runs a new ad. Usually, you can preview the sales by waiting until 24 hours before the next ad starts so you can compare the two to figure out what you should buy at which point in the week. It takes a little planning, but once it becomes the norm, those savings add up.

Search through Coupons

Another great way to save some cash is to pay attention to the coupons offered to you by the store. There's a good chance that you can save cash on some items when you do this. It may not be the most efficient way of saving money, but if you're determined to cut down on costs, this is another strategy to include—especially if you wait to use the coupons until they can be used in tandem with the weekly sales.

Stick to the List

You might start seeing other foods and things that you think are worth picking up, but not adhering to a list is usually how shopping trips end up costing significantly more than you intended to spend. By going to the store with a plan in mind and sticking to buying only what you had on your list when you entered the store, you can help to reduce your bill. This is because when you stick to your list, you're able to ensure you're getting the best price possible for an item before you choose to purchase it, by waiting and then cross-comparing with other stores.

Check Several Stores

Before committing to purchasing something, it's a good idea to look through the weekly ads of several stores and shop at multiple places. Sometimes, the prices may warrant stopping at several stores instead of just shopping at one.

Check the Price per Unit of Everything

The price per unit is a way that you can compare the prices to see which size is providing you with the most for the least amount of money. Before you choose to buy anything, always compare the price per unit. Usually, you get a better price per unit by buying in bulk, but this is not a hard and fast rule. Sometimes, smaller quantities are cheaper.

GARDENING FOR YOUR FOOD STOCKPILE

If land is no issue for you, you might establish a garden. Using a garden to add to your food stockpile is a great way for you to be certain that you've got fresh food. The food that you grow can then be canned and preserved, or frozen, to make sure that you've got additional food available to you. If you've got plenty of space available, certain foods that will last longer in your pantry can be gardened readily.

You may live somewhere that growing food year-round is entirely possible. You may even grow indoors, using hydroponics and grow lights, or in a greenhouse that will help you grow food even when the temperatures are too cold outdoors. However, these aren't always workable options for all people, especially when you're in an urban or suburban area. If you've got a plot of land and you're not doing much with it at the moment, creating a garden that can sustain you is a great way to ensure that you're stockpiling food at very little cost to you.

As you stock your pantry and freezer with produce, the best thing you can do is select foods that are easier to store because they keep for months when kept cool and dry, or because you can pickle, can, or freeze them.

Vegetables that can simply be stored in cool, dry places include:

- Dried beans
- Garlic
- Onions
- Potatoes
- Pumpkin
- Shallots
- Sweet potatoes
- Winter squash

Vegetables that may be canned easily in sealable glass jars include:

- Asparagus
- Beans
- Beets
- Carrots
- Cabbage
- Corn
- Peas
- Peppers
- Pickled onions
- Pickled cucumbers
- Potatoes
- Tomatoes
- Winter squash

If you want to stock a deep freezer with the vegetables you've grown, you can grow crops such as:

- Asparagus
- Broccoli
- Brussels sprouts
- Cabbage
- Carrots
- Cauliflower
- Corn

- Eggplant
- Mushrooms
- Onions
- Peas
- Spinach
- Squash
- Tomatoes (when processed)

We will address how to store vegetables later in the book. However, with so many options available to you for the storage of your vegetables, having a garden of your own could be a valuable way to create your stockpile at home.

Gardening in Small Spaces

Even if you've got less space available to you than you'd like, there are ways you can garden in smaller spaces with little trouble. By focusing on using the space that you have, you will enjoy the benefits of gardening, even if it's on a smaller scale.

Vertical Gardens

Vertical gardens are those that primarily grow upwards. This is done by growing on a vertical plane instead of a horizontal one. Typically, several planters are placed slightly on an angle so you can grow several tiers of something in a row. These usually work well for plants that grow somewhat smaller, such as some greens, herbs, carrots, and other small vegetables.

Raised Beds

Raised beds allow you to create a small area dedicated solely to gardening. Usually, they are in sizes like 2'x4' or 4'x4', and you can fill them up with soil, allowing you to grow even if you live somewhere that doesn't have very good ground for growing, such as if you have a small patio with little soil.

Container Planting

If you don't even have the space for a raised bed, there are plenty of containers you can plant in. Many plants can be grown in containers, including fruit trees. You can grow, for example, a pot of tomatoes and pick them throughout the season. You could grow a container of peas or carrots, or just about anything else. Most plants can be grown in a container, as long as you're willing to care for them properly. Often, because container planting involves so much less space than other forms of gardening, you'll need to be mindful of how you choose to care for them. They will need to be watered and fertilized more often, but you can still get plenty of produce from them.

Potted Fruit Trees

Potted fruit trees often do well, especially if you select dwarf varieties and you keep them trimmed. You'll be able to get plenty of fruits from them, however, so don't discount them for their small size. Just keep in mind that many fruits require at least two trees of the same species to properly fertilize and fruit.

FEMA RECOMMENDATIONS

So how much food should you have on hand? This depends on what you're trying to prepare for. Do you want to ensure that you've got food just in case of a storm, or are you trying to prepare for another wave of massive lockdowns? The answer will be based on that. While most preppers will strive to have six months to a year of food on hand, the current recommendation from FEMA is at least three days' worth of non-perishable food on hand at all times, which is a good place to start and build from there. In particular, they recommend that you have:

- At least three days' worth of non-perishable foods
- Foods your family will enjoy eating, especially if you have picky children
- Foods that meet all special dietary requirements

- Foods that won't make you thirsty, such as dried foods or foods high in salt

In particular, they recommend items such as:

- Canned juices
- Comfort foods (in moderation)
- Dried fruits
- Dry cereals
- Granola
- High-energy foods
- Infant foods (if applicable)
- Non-perishable milk (pasteurized)
- Peanut butter
- Protein and fruit bars
- Ready-to-eat canned goods (fruits, vegetables, and meat, with a manual can opener on hand)

Because you have no way of knowing whether whatever emergency comes your way will include power outages or other such disasters, it's always a good idea to ensure that you've got foods that will not need to be prepared. Of course, it's important to have other foods on hand as well.

Why You Should Have at Least 30 Days' Worth of Food

While FEMA provides a general guideline for short-term emergencies, what happens on a larger scale? What if you can't get to the store? What if there is a long-term disaster? Wuhan, China locked down for 76 days because of COVID-19, with strong limits on who could go outdoors and when. The quarantine was severe enough that people were stuck at home, and when they could get out, stores were often short on supplies.

Three days is a good start to a stockpile for immediate emergencies, but if you worry that you or your household will be stuck at home for a longer time, having significantly more is a good idea. You'll want to start your stockpile with the intention of having 30 days' worth of food and water on hand at all times. Once you have your 30-day supply, it's a lot easier to build on your stocks and slowly build up your stores.

You might think this sounds easy: Couldn't you just buy a bunch of crackers, soup, and rice and call it good? While you would probably survive, you wouldn't be doing your health any favors. You want to make sure that you've got 30 days' worth of nutritious, whole foods that will keep your body healthy even when you can't get out and shop as normal. If you don't plan well, you could wind up with an unsustainable diet that leaves you and your family feeling sick and miserable. You can prevent this relatively easily if you take the time to plan well.

This is essential, especially in this day and age. Anything could happen. The world is teetering on war, with new conflicts seeming to arise every year as others appear to go away. We are in the midst of a massive climate change that could decimate crops. There is the possibility of an earthquake destroying transportation infrastructure. When the supply line falls apart, it will take a significant amount of time to get it working again. What this means for you is that you need to have plenty of food on hand at any point in time.

Canned Meat and Fish

Protein is essential to your body, and if you don't have enough of it, you're going to struggle with ensuring that you've got everything you need to stay healthy. When you select canned meats, it's important to choose grass-fed when possible, and to choose high-quality products that are going to keep you full and nourished. They may not taste as good as fresh or frozen, but in a pinch, they will help you survive, and that's what this is about. For a month, you will probably want to keep around 35 cans of various meats on hand, assuming you have a family of two or three. If you've got a larger family, you may need to double this, as one can only contains about three servings.

Chicken

Canned chicken is easy to find at any supermarket, often in varying sizes of cans. As we discussed, chicken supports the immune system while also reducing inflammation, which helps you to avoid illness and gives you extra support when you're sick. Vitamin B6 will also aid in the development of healthy red blood cells.

Tuna

Tuna is a rich source of omega-3 fatty acids, as well as other fats and oils. Tuna can also be dressed up in many meals, making it quite versatile. If you buy it packed in oil, you keep the flavor and have some extra fat available to use too.

Salmon

Like tuna, salmon is great for providing omega-3 fatty acids. It is also rich in selenium. Salmon is usually a bit more expensive than tuna, however, so make sure that you plan accordingly.

Red Meat

Red meats will provide you with plenty of zinc, which you also need for your immune system. When possible, find grass-fed options.

Canned Vegetables

Canned vegetables are a substantial source of vitamins if you can't find them fresh. It's a good idea to prioritize getting starchy vegetables, such as root veggies and sweet potatoes, as they'll provide you with more calories per ounce than many other options. They're also usually still quite rich in vitamins and minerals to keep you healthy. You'll need around 40 cans, at a minimum, to last a month. You should get whatever you and your family will eat, with an emphasis on:

- Asparagus
- Carrots
- Mushrooms
- Spinach

Canned Fruits

Fruits are an essential part of your diet, and you can usually stockpile them relatively easily in canned form. If you have access to refrigeration, you can refrigerate the leftovers of larger cans and buy the #10 cans, which contain 25 servings each. You and your family will enjoy one to two servings per day relatively cheaply in this manner. Ideally, you'll choose a variety for the most health benefits, but in particular, you want to make sure you have canned grapefruit in there somewhere for its immune-boosting properties.

There's a big debate around whether you want to purchase fruits packed in syrup or juice. A lot of preppers support the idea of buying in syrup as it has a higher calorie content with the additional sugar provided. However, to emphasize and prioritize health, it's better to select fruits that have been canned in their juices instead.

Honey

Honey is a great sweetener with medicinal properties. It is used commonly in teas to boost immune system support, and in medical emergencies, its antibacterial properties can help promote wound healing if you have no other options available to you.

When stored correctly, honey never goes bad. Keep it dry and cool, and you'll be safe. You can buy this in bulk and use it slowly, using it in place of sugar or to add some flavor to oatmeal or yogurt.

SALT, HERBS, AND SPICES

If you were to only eat unseasoned food from cans, you'd probably get sick of it pretty quickly. With no variety, you're bound to get bored. This is where salts, herbs, and spices come into play. You want to make sure that you've got plenty of all three on hand.

Salt for Food Preservation

Salt, in particular, will never go bad when kept dry, and it can add flavor to just about anything with a quick sprinkle. You can get it incredibly cheaply, and it provides essential sodium that your body requires.

Salt can also preserve your food. It's recommended that, in addition to table salt, you have pink Himalayan salt on hand. This salt, although more expensive, is rich in trace minerals that your body needs.

Herbs and Spices

Many herbs and spices also provide you with plenty of health benefits on top of flavor. In particular, try to keep turmeric, ginger, and cinnamon on hand. Not only are they incredibly flavorful to make your food more enjoyable, but they're also jam-packed with benefits. Ginger and turmeric support the immune system, while cinnamon is known for controlling blood sugar and having anti-inflammatory properties.

Garlic

Garlic can be kept for a few months in a pantry or some other cool, dry place. However, if you're hoping for something to last longer, you can buy it dehydrated in a powdered form, pickled, frozen, or canned. All varieties will add a massive amount of flavor to any dish, while also allowing you to benefit from the immune boost.

Hard Cheeses

Cheese is a great option for adding flavor, calories, convenience, and even some health benefits. Cheese has been popular for millennia, and it's worthy of a place in the prepper's stockpile. However, only certain cheeses are suitable for long-term storage. Cheeses come in either soft, semi-soft, or hard options. Hard cheeses are suitable for long-term storage because they have had their moisture extracted. Then, when freeze-dried or dehydrated, it can last even longer.

Hard cheeses can outlast the canned goods in your pantry, so long as they're stored well and they're unopened. Hard cheeses you can keep on hand include:

- Cheddar
- Gouda
- Parmesan
- Romano

You'll want to ensure that there is wax coating the cheese to ensure that moisture cannot get into it and cause it to go bad. With no way for moisture to get to the cheese, there's not much risk in keeping it. Some cheeses are aged for decades before they are even sold, so aim to keep a lot of these options on hand. You could also choose powdered cheese to mix into pastas and potatoes or coat meats, or even cheese in a can or jar.

Cereals

Having some cereals on hand is a great way to ensure that you can get a quick boost of energy, so long as you get the good stuff. Now's not the time to run out and stockpile sugary cereal: It's time to choose foods that you know are going to do your body some favors without making you feel ill along the way. Plus, cereals are a cheaper substitute for many other foods you could buy. Try to stock up at least five big boxes to ensure you've got enough. Your cereals should be:

- Whole-grain varieties with no added sugars.
- From a variety of different grain bases to ensure you're getting all the nutritional value you need.

Many cereals these days are fortified with many of the vitamins and minerals people are deficient in, so while cereal may not be the healthiest option for you, it's also not the worst thing you could eat. And, by adding wheat germ, you can fortify the cereal with more fiber, vitamin E, protein, folate, magnesium, zinc, selenium, and manganese.

Canned Soups

Canned soups may not be the most nutritious option for you, but they last a long time, making them a prepper's favorite. When you have canned soups in stock, they can provide a great emergency backup if you run out of other food. Make sure that whatever soups you choose, you emphasize the healthier ones with higher vegetable content and many ingredients to ensure that you're getting a variety of vitamins and minerals.

Nuts and Seeds

Nuts and seeds are calorically dense and loaded with healthy fats and energy. You can get plenty of nutrients just from nuts while filling in the bulk of your calories, or you could choose to mix them with oatmeal or cereal for an additional crunch. You can use them in many forms. However, it's recommended that you prioritize both almonds and sunflower seeds. If you can, select them in bags rather than jars.

Apple Cider Vinegar

Apple cider vinegar is antimicrobial and also commonly used to help reduce cholesterol, manage diabetes, and lower blood sugar levels. It's good for gut health, and may even aid in weight loss. Because of how it is processed, it is full of many probiotics, but it is quite acidic and should be consumed diluted in water.

Vinegar may also treat wounds, nail fungus, lice, warts, and ear infections, and it can also help preserve food for longer. Having a bottle or two on hand in your pantry is strongly recommended.

Leavening Agents

There's a good chance that you'll want to make bread in an emergency situation, and if you want that bread to rise, you'll need leavening agents. The most common are baking soda, baking powder, and active dry yeast, which has a longer shelf life than the fresh stuff. Keeping these on hand means that you should be able to make many baked goods with little trouble.

Butter

Butter is essential to many cuisines, and let's be real: it tastes good, too! Plus, the health benefits are worth it. Not only is it full of calories, which you'll need for energy, it's also rich in many other essential vitamins and minerals. If you can, get grass-fed options and store them in your freezer to lengthen the life span.

Shopping for your stash of food can be intimidating, especially if you're already on a budget. However, you don't have to buy everything all at once, and you don't have to buy exactly what's on this list. What has been provided here are general guidelines to help you piece together a stockpile that will suit your family's needs. Use this list to plan your shopping to build up little by little.

Chapter Summary

In this chapter, we went over the first wave of what you should have in your pantry and why you need it.

- Stockpiling doesn't have to be expensive if you play your cards right and shop smarter.
- You should have at least 30 days' worth of food stocked up in order to be prepared for any disasters.
- Your stockpile should contain an assortment of canned fruits, vegetables, meats, herbs, spices, fats, nuts, and grains.
- If you want to be able to keep your supplies topped up, gardening is a good way to supplement your stockpile.

4

BULK SHOPPING FOR LONG-TERM STORAGE, SURVIVAL, AND OPTIMUM HEALTH

Y ou might think that your canned goods will be enough for your family to get by on, and you might be right, but you're probably not going to be getting the balanced diet that your body requires if you rely on cans alone. You still need to have a stockpile of the essential macronutrients found in foods such as rice, beans, lentils, and oatmeal to ensure that you can get the caloric content you need without going hungry.

This chapter will essentially supplement the high-calorie and nice-to-haves that you'll want to keep in your pantry.

These foods will probably come in much larger packages, and you'll most likely need to break them down to store them. Otherwise, you risk having an entire bag contaminated if something goes wrong, and when you're talking about large amounts of food, that can be devastating. You'll most likely want to shop from bulk wholesalers or online to get larger packages and save some money.

The biggest mistake I see people making is seeing a prepper pantry list and buying all the items, even if they don't like them. So just remember that this is a guide: Only buy food that you and your family both enjoy and eat regularly.

Rice

Rice has been a human staple for centuries for a reason. It's easy to produce, easy to cook, and can fill you up rapidly. It can also be stored long-term with little problem. The most economical way to buy rice is to buy it in 40-pound bags, which you can then pack into buckets to protect it from bugs or rodents that might find it easy to chew through the bags.

Brown rice is higher in nutritional content and fiber than many other options. However, it doesn't last as long as white rice. It's a great option to keep on hand for fiber or health reasons, but also stock white basmati rice, which is healthy and will last longer.

Beans and Lentils

You can buy beans in 5-gallon buckets already packaged for you, but you can usually get a discount if you buy the large bags and move them into buckets yourself. Ideally, you'll have several types of beans to get a wider range of nutrition. Beans and lentils offer a significant source of energy and vegetarian protein, and if you're worried about running out of them, you can sprout them rapidly to get your stock going again, especially if you've got space to garden.

Oatmeal

Oatmeal can also be purchased in bulk. A 5-gallon bucket contains around 222 servings. If you don't want to buy in bulk, a normal container usually has around 30 servings, so for a family of four, you'll want to buy at least four of them for a month. Oatmeal is also much more filling than many other breakfast option. You can even flavor it with honey, fruit, nuts, or anything else, if you want additional staying power and to make it enjoyable.

Oatmeal is highly regarded thanks to being both beneficial to the immune system and having a high fiber content. That, paired with the slow release of energy you get, thanks to oatmeal being a complex carb, makes this a great option for a stockpile.

Pasta

Pasta is a substantial addition to many meals, and you can add tomato sauce easily to pack a nutritional punch. When you keep pasta, look for dried varieties, which have very little moisture content which allows them to be kept long-term. Ideally, you'll select whole-grain varieties to get the best nutritional value out of them. You can buy these in boxes or bags and store them. Try to have at least 5–10 boxes on hand. You can usually find them in bulk packages online or in warehouses.

Sugar

Sugar doesn't offer many nutritional benefits. However, what it has is energy. While it shouldn't be a staple that you consume all the time, it is helpful in cooking and baking, and it is quite effective in an emergency when you need something to provide enough calories. Sugar can be stored easily, and you can buy it in bulk. Storing it in 5-gallon buckets is the perfect way to keep it safe.

Dehydrated Milk and Eggs

While you'll hopefully have access to milk and eggs in most situations, if you find yourself locked down for longer than a few weeks, you may end up running out of them. Eggs can usually keep for about a month in the fridge, or much longer if you crack and freeze them like ice cubes, but milk is usually only good for a short period before it goes bad. This is why having dehydrated milk and eggs on hand is a good idea.

Dehydrated eggs usually come in powdered form, and by adding some water to them, you can create an egg mixture that you can use for scrambled eggs. You could also toss them in as powder while baking for significant results. Because of the nutritional value of eggs, it's a good idea to include them in your stockpile.

Milk is great for calcium, and by having powdered milk on hand, you can add some water to it and have the benefits you'd get from drinking milk in a cup. You could use this for cooking as well.

Powdered Whey

Sometimes referred to as whey protein, this is a staple for many bodybuilders because of its high protein content. It can be mixed into drinks to not only flavor them, but also to provide a boost of nutrition. If you're low on protein, adding this to your milk is a great way to fortify it. You can usually find powdered whey in gallon-sized containers and it comes in many flavors.

Drink Mixes

Water is essential to drink to ensure you're healthy, but sometimes, people get bored with it. It's a good idea to have other options on hand as well, such as tea and coffee. Coffee is an excellent caffeine source, and if you're already used to drinking it, you probably don't want to run out of it and deal with caffeine withdrawal. Coffee is also known to be good for the heart, in moderation, and is rich in immune-boosting antioxidants.

Teas typically infuse water with many medicinal properties. In particular, you want to focus on:

- **Chamomile:** Chamomile is the classic tea people turn to when they've got a cold, and for good reason. It's been used for centuries to aid the immune system while also providing relief from cold symptoms. It also helps you to relax. It is commonly served with honey, which also brings soothing benefits.
- **Echinacea:** Echinacea, sometimes referred to as purple coneflower, is a popular tea that was used regularly by Native Americans. These days, it is an herbal treatment for the cold or flu. It may help with inflammation and migraines as well.
- **Ginger:** Ginger tea transforms the antimicrobial benefits of ginger into drinkable form, boosting your immune system. This tea is sweet and spicy, but it's delicious.

- **Hibiscus:** Hibiscus teas are typically filled with antibacterial and antimicrobial properties to help aid in fending off illness while boosting health. It's also rich in iron, antioxidants, and vitamin C.
- **Lemon balm:** Lemon balm smells lemony and delivers significant benefits. It is used for boosting mood and cognitive function, while also boosting your immune system. It is commonly used to relieve nausea, headaches, and menstrual cramps, making it a great tea to keep on hand.
- **Peppermint:** Peppermint tea may be drunk on its own, or as an ingredient in an herbal blend. The mintiness is perfect for soothing a sore throat, and it is rich in antioxidants, also offering antimicrobial benefits.
- **Rooibos:** Rooibos tea is a traditional African tea that is quickly becoming more popular worldwide. It is flavorful and caffeine-free, while also boasting a high antioxidant content.
- **Sage:** Sage tea is known for being laden with anti-inflammatory and antioxidant compounds that may also aid in wound healing. It also is rich in vitamin K.

Oils

Oils are typically used for cooking, but some offer very good health benefits as well. Coconut and olive oils are both highly recommended. Most of the time, rich, hearty flavors come from fat content, and most meals require you to use some sort of fat, whether oil or butter. Having oil on hand is essential for your stock-pile. Keep in mind that oil has a limited lifespan: Olive oil, for example, doesn't last nearly as long as you'd think, so make sure you're constantly pulling from your stockpile and cycling through new products. It is only good for between 12 and 18 months, at which point it goes rancid. Keep an enormous bottle on hand at all times, but to avoid waste, don't go too crazy on your stockpile.

Extra virgin olive oil is unrefined, meaning it is of higher quality. It is higher in monounsaturated fats that have been linked to better heart health. However, keep in mind that it has a low smoke point, which means it can't be used for cooking at very high temperatures.

Coconut oil lasts longer, but should be used in moderation. It is high in saturated fats, which is okay if you're not eating too much of it. It is still a healthy option, full of antioxidants, and it is highly versatile. It can be used for cooking, as a lotion, and to clean and condition hair, amongst other things. It is also more tolerant of higher cooking temperatures. You can find this in 5-gallon buckets to stockpile.

Flour

Flour is essential for baking unless you can't tolerate the gluten within it. Having flour on hand will be required for most people, however. You'll need this for baking, making easy meals like pancakes, or even for making your pasta, which is much easier than you'd think if you're in a pinch.

When you select your flours, select a variety. It's always a good idea to have some all-purpose flour on hand, but you also want to keep whole-grain flours as well. You can grind down your oatmeal into oatmeal flour as well.

However, keep in mind that flours are easy to ruin. A bit of moisture will cause them to spoil quickly. Flour should be stored carefully, somewhere airtight and waterproof, with oxygen absorbers. We'll talk more about this later.

Households should have roughly 50 pounds of flour per person for a year-long supply. If you want enough for a month, you'd want between 4 and 5 pounds per person.

Potato Flour

Potato flour is another good option to have on hand. Typically, it's made from the entire potato, which provides you with plenty of benefits. It is often used to stretch regular flour, or you can use it to bake with as well. It's a common thickener when making sauces and gravies, thanks to the starch.

Dried Fruits

We've already touched on canned fruits, but it's a good idea to keep some dried fruits on hand as well. You can buy them in buckets or large cans, and many varieties come with a lot of benefits. Raisins, for example, are full of protein, iron, fiber, potassium, and vitamin C. However, keep in mind that dried fruits often have higher concentrations of sugar since they've been dehydrated and lost much of their bulk. It's very easy to eat too much sugar if you're not careful. Select several types of dried fruits for the best benefits.

Freeze-Dried Chicken

We discussed the benefits of canned chicken in Chapter 3. In freeze-dried form, it includes many of those same benefits, and you can buy this in bulk just as easily. It is often sold in large cans, and by adding boiling water to the chicken, you can rehydrate it to enjoy when you need it. You can buy this in large #10 cans.

Having a fully-stocked pantry is essential. It's strongly recommended that whenever you shop, you keep up with your pantry, always ensuring you have at least one, but preferably up to six months' worth of essential ingredients on hand. Many of these foods can be used regularly, like rice, flour, and oatmeal. Other foods should only be kept on hand for emergency occurrences, such as powdered eggs or milk. Ensuring that you have a well-replenished pantry will keep you healthy and provide you with plenty to fall back on in times of shortage.

Chapter Summary

In this chapter, we finished going over foods that should be stocked in a pantry at all times for a one-month reserve of food.

- Grains such as rice, oatmeal, and flour should be stored well and kept for a source of carbohydrates.
- Herbal teas can be highly beneficial for medicinal purposes.
- Baking supplies, such as powdered eggs and milk, as well as oils, will help stretch out the meals.
- Dried foods, such as fruits and chicken, can help save space and boost the longevity of food.

5

STORING DRY FOODS: EVERYTHING YOU NEED TO KNOW ABOUT CONTAINERS

Once you start stockpiling your food, you'll probably notice that there's a lot of dry foods that need to be stored. Storing dry foods isn't as simple as just tossing them in the containers that they came in into your pantry. You need to make sure you protect them from light, insects, rodents, oxygen, and moisture.

When foods that are low in fat and moisture are stored properly, they can be stored for much longer than you might think. Wheat from 4,000 years ago was found in an Egyptian tomb, and it was still edible. This was because it was stored properly.

Since the whole point of storing food is to protect your family if you cannot access normal grocery shopping for an extended period, you want to make sure it is protected. Without the proper care, you may find that the foods you thought you could rely on are no longer good. Most packaging lasts for about a year, but if you want to keep foods for longer, you'll want to ensure that they have been cared for the right way.

Whether you're packing grains or legumes, there are a few simple steps you can follow to ensure they're suitable candidates. These are:

1. Choose high-quality dry foods that contain less than 10% moisture and are also low in oil content, such as white rice.
2. Select the right container for the food, the space you have, and your preference.
3. Choose the best method to prevent insects from infesting the container.

While you might be a bit intimidated by all of this, it's not as hard as you might think. As you get more familiar with the options, choosing the right one becomes almost intuitive. By following these guidelines, you will be able to keep your food safe so you know you can rely on it when it's time.

As you read through this chapter, you will be introduced to several key topics that will assist you in storing your dry foods. We will first cover what makes your storage choices effective. Then we will go over the most common options: Mylar bags, cans, PET bottles, plastic buckets, and glass jars. We will address how to treat your containers in several ways, and finally cover how you can store your food to keep it safe.

WHAT MAKES A CONTAINER EFFECTIVE?

Food containers must be effective, or you're just wasting your money. If you want to ensure that you're choosing the most effective containers, you need something that's going to prevent your food from spoiling. Most foods will spoil because they're contaminated with something. Typically, this is air, chemicals, insects, light, moisture, rodents, temperature, or time. Now, most of these can be mitigated in other ways. Time is controlled by rotating your stores regularly. Temperature and moisture are eliminated by using a cool, dry pantry for your storage. Chemical contamination is avoided by using only food-grade products to store everything. This leaves your container needing to combat against just four of the biggest spoilers of your food: oxygen, light, insects, and rodents.

Blocks Oxygen

The air you breathe contains roughly 21% oxygen, which allows it to oxidize many compounds in food. It also allows for both insects and bacteria to grow. By removing or displacing oxygen, you can help boost the shelf life of the foods you choose to store. This means that your most effective containers will have some way of blocking airflow from entering. Throwing an oxygen absorber into the container will also be useful for longer shelf life.

Blocks Light

Light can cause changes to the physical and chemical properties of your food. In particular, it allows for food to deteriorate rapidly and causes the degradation of nutrients. It can also degrade the packaging, so if you think you can get away with storing your rice in a bucket that doesn't allow light to enter, you're wrong: The container will still degrade. The best thing you can do is ensure that where you place the container is dark.

Blocks Insects

Insects would love nothing more than to get into the stockpiles you set up. Once they invade, there's going to be no way to decontaminate the food they get into. Insects will enter your grain stores if you keep them in their original packaging, which is why it's such a good idea to store them in something else.

The most common pests that you're likely to run into are weevils, beetles, moths, and ants. They'll do whatever they can to get into your food. They will go from egg to larva to pupa to adult, and it's difficult to eliminate them once they're able to spread. The best thing you can do is to store your food somewhere oxygen-free, which will deprive the insects of necessary air and keep your food safe.

Blocks Rodents

Mice are troublesome, as they can chew through foil pouches and Mylar bags rapidly. They can even chew through plastic buckets if they're determined to do so. Rats can be even worse: They can even get through metal containers if they're determined enough. If you've got rodents, there's a good chance they're going to target your food store. You will need to keep the environment clean and free from rodents. If they're able to chew their way into the bag, they will contaminate your food stocks.

TYPES OF CONTAINERS

Mylar Bags

Mylar bags are made of multilayer laminated plastic and aluminum. Because the food is separated from aluminum by a food-grade plastic layer, there is little risk of contamination. These bags are effective at protecting food from moisture and insects, but they allow for a small amount of oxygen to enter, and they are not rodent-proof. If you want to use Mylar, it's usually a good idea to place those bags into a bucket of some sort to protect them from rodent damage.

Typically, these bags can last up to 5 years, or 20 if you add oxygen absorbers and vacuum seal them. Each gallon of food should use one 300 cc oxygen absorber or 2,000 cc oxygen absorbers per 5-gallon bucket.

Make sure that when you use Mylar bags, you use a heat-sealing device to seal them entirely. If you want to vacuum seal them and secure them using a traditional vacuum sealing device you already have, you can do that too. This requires a bit of creativity, but if you know what you're doing, you can make it work well.

Mylar bags are typically smooth, while vacuum-sealing bags have textured sides to allow channels to be created for the vacuum sealer to suck the air through. By taking a few snips out of your bags, you'll be able to create those channels on your Mylar bag as well. Put two small snips, maybe 1 inch by 2 inches long, on each corner of the Mylar bag, with maybe a ½ inch sticking out the top. Place it into your vacuum sealer, and allow it to suck out all the air. This will take longer than you'd normally expect vacuum sealing to work since there will only be two small channels to use, but it should suck out all the air. At that point, you can use the heat seal setting. Do this twice, and your bag should be secure and ready to go.

Mylar bags should be kept in some other container to prevent them from coming into direct contact with cement or walls. Keep in mind that these bags don't stack well, so they can be a bit of a mess to store well. Your best bet is to store them in large 5-gallon bags, and place these in large square buckets.

Keep in mind that foods with over 10% moisture content risk developing botulism in a low-oxygen environment, so make sure that you only pack dried goods, such as rice, beans, pasta, oats, flour, and sugar. Freeze-dried foods will also do well, but you want to avoid foods rich in oil or moisture.

Cans

If you need to store foods that are low-oil content, dry, and shelf-stable, cans are a great option. However, you must make sure that there is an enamel coating between the food and the metal to keep it food-safe. Cans are traditionally kept in most stockpiles. However, make sure that you have a manual can opener if you choose to stock up in this manner.

Like Mylar bags, it's recommended to use low-moisture foods to prevent reaction with the metal. While a lot of liquid foods may come in cans, they are not suitable for longer-term storage. When possible, dry foods should be stored with oxygen absorbers, except for sugar.

Unlike Mylar bags, however, these can prevent all oxygen from entering the cans. They can rust on the outside, though, so you want to keep them somewhere without moisture. They should not be kept in direct contact with concrete. Typically, you can use a rolling rack to store your cans. Just make sure you label them so you can tell what's in each can.

A #10 can holds 3 quarts and is good for 2.8 pounds of rolled oats, 3 pounds of macaroni, or 5.5 pounds of pinto beans. It may store other foods as well, and you can open them in much smaller amounts than if they were stored in large buckets.

Polyethylene Terephthalate (PET) Bottles

Polyethylene terephthalate (PET) bottles can be good options if you're running low on other types of storage. You should only use PET bottles if you're storing dry goods, however, as they don't provide much of a moisture barrier.

To identify which bottles you have that are PET, look for the number "1" in the recycle symbol. It may also say "PETE" or "PET" underneath the symbol. These bottles should have a screw-on lid, which should also have a plastic or rubber seal. For example, 2-liter soda bottles are made in this manner. You can reuse these; just make sure they're cleaned and dried well. If you've ever used the bottle for non-food purposes, don't reuse it.

You can store rice, corn, beans, and wheat in these bottles for a longer-term period, or you can use them short-term for other foods as well. If you are storing long-term, use one oxygen absorber packet per bottle. Keep in mind that these options must be kept protected from light and rodents. These options aren't as efficient as Mylar or canning, but they are still effective in a pinch.

Plastic Buckets

Using large plastic buckets is another great option, but you must make sure that they are food-grade. They must also be free from other food items. If you've used them for non-food items in the past, don't use them. You can either store food in its original packaging for added protection, or you can choose to use the bucket itself to store things with liners.

Buckets are typically the recommended options for storing food long-term in larger quantities, but keep in mind that oxygen can enter them. It's a good idea to use Mylar bags to line them. Then, make sure you store them off the floor without stacking more than three buckets on top of each other in order to protect the seals.

Grains, flour, sugar, and other dried foods store well in these containers. They are also among the least expensive options for sealing. Just keep in mind that you should only choose food with gaskets in the lid seals.

Glass Jars

If you want to store smaller quantities of something, using glass jars is one of the most effective ways to do so. Their smaller sizes make them convenient, and they can be reused several times, so long as you don't accidentally drop and break them. They are both air and watertight, making them quite efficient, and rodents can't chew through them without significant difficulty and injury. However, because glass is transparent, you need to keep it protected from light in order to prolong the life of your food.

TREATMENT OPTIONS

Before you store anything in a container, one of the most important things you can do is make sure that there's no chance of an insect infestation. Eggs are often too small for you to see, and you may not notice if there are a few tiny insects in a big bag of rice as you pour it into a container. The best thing you can do is use some sort of treatment to protect your food stores. Typically, this is done through a method that will help to reduce oxygen content, which will both kill anything hiding in the food and expand your food's shelf life.

There are a few options you can choose from, and it's worth familiarizing yourself with all of them. The options you have are dry ice, oxygen absorbers, diatomaceous earth, and desiccants or silica gel.

Dry Ice

Sometimes, the best treatment to rid your food of any bugs is to use dry ice. This is frozen carbon dioxide, which, as it thaws out, will displace oxygen because it is heavier. This means that when you fill up a bucket with carbon dioxide, it will remain there, as it is heavier than the surrounding air. So if you want to remove oxygen from a large container environment, such as in a 5-gallon bucket, dry ice is highly effective. It is particularly recommended if you choose to store grains and legumes in any large plastic buckets.

To treat your bucket, you will need an ounce of dry ice for every gallon. In a 5-gallon bucket, 4 ounces should suffice. Clean off any ice crystals that have been collected on the dry ice. Then, wrap it in a paper towel so it won't burn any food it comes into contact with. Put the wrapped ice on the bottom of the container and pour your grains or beans on top of it. There should be an inch of leeway at the top of the container. Attach the lid, only sealing half of it, so that the carbon dioxide can escape as the ice sublimates from the solid into gas form. This will usually take around an hour. Seal the bucket once you're sure the ice has sublimated completely. At that point, wait and see if the lid has bulged at all. If it does, release the pressure by opening the lid. Your lid should pull downward slightly to show a partial vacuum effect, and this is how you will know you've done your job properly. As the carbon dioxide is absorbed into the food, it pulls the lid down.

Oxygen Absorbers

Oxygen absorbers are usually quite effective at removing oxygen from containers, allowing them to kill insects in adult or larval form. Oxygen absorber pouches are small packets of iron powder. Oxygen and moisture can enter the packet, but the iron powder cannot leak out. The moisture in the food causes the iron to rust, and during the oxidation process, it absorbs the oxygen as well. These are highly recommended, and often more effective than vacuum packaging.

However, keep in mind that botulism may grow in high-moisture and low-oxygen environments, so make sure you only use these for low-moisture products. Use them in containers with sufficient moisture and oxygen barriers, like #10 cans, Mylar pouches, and glass canning jars. Avoid using oxygen absorbers with:

- Brown rice
- Dehydrated fruits and vegetables that won't snap when bent
- Dried eggs
- Granola

- Jerky
- Leavening agents (they may explode)
- Milled grains
- Nuts
- Pearl barley
- Salt and sugar (they turn hard with an oxygen absorber)

Different-sized containers will need different amounts of oxygen absorbers. As a general rule, use the following guidelines:

- Use 100 cc for quarts or smaller
- Use 400 cc absorbers for between a quart and a gallon
- Use 400 ccs per gallon for containers between 1 and 5 gallons
- Use a 3,000 cc for 5- and 6-gallon buckets

These guidelines err on the side of a little too much rather than not enough, because using a little extra won't do anything to your food, but not using enough is going to allow pests or bacteria to develop, or will pose a risk to the nutrition content of your food.

To use oxygen absorbers, follow these steps:

1. Prepare the containers and ensure they're entirely dry with the lid nearby.
2. Prepare the food, making sure it's free from debris, and place it in the containers.
3. Place the oxygen absorbers in a tightly closed mason jar while you're not using them. Open the jar and pull out as much as you need. Make sure it feels soft and powdery. If it feels hard or chunky, it will not absorb any more. It should also feel warm to the touch: They are warm when they're absorbing oxygen.
4. Seal the container rapidly as soon the oxygen absorber is inside.
5. Label with the date of packaging, and wait a few days or a week. Keep in mind that they absorb oxygen and not air, so it won't look fully vacuum-sealed, but it should look smaller. If it doesn't look smaller, open it up and add more, repeating the process.

Diatomaceous Earth

Diatomaceous earth is created from the fossilized remains of marine diatoms. These microscopic remains have sharp spines all over them, which can cut into insects with exoskeletons. These wounds allow for moisture to be lost from the insect, and the insects then die. People and animals typically are not negatively affected by it. However, to ensure your safety, you must make sure that you've chosen a food-grade option, rather than the kind used in swimming pool filters. You can usually find it in garden centers, hardware stores, or feed stores without too much issue.

This product is best used by taking 1 cup of diatomaceous earth to mix thoroughly into 40 pounds of grain, grain products, or legumes. Be mindful that this option is only effective against adult insects, so you still want to be as safe as possible to prevent infestation. Also keep in mind that diatomaceous earth is a dust, so it would be wise to use a mask and avoid breathing it in during the mixing process to avoid irritating your lungs.

Desiccant / Silica Gel

Desiccant will remove the moisture in the surrounding air, allowing you to create a low-moisture environment. It removes humidity to prevent the development of rust, mold, mildew, fungus, corrosion, or oxidation. It is regularly used both in food storage and in manufactured products.

Commonly, you'll find silica gel packaged in Tyvek, which meets the FDA requirement as a safe option for dry food packing. You can layer several packets throughout the container, and seal up the container immediately after. Make sure you discard the packets as soon as you open the container.

Some options may be rechargeable, so to speak, if you expose them to heat to allow them to release oxygen, but make sure you don't do this without verifying whether the type you have works this way. Silica gel is inedible, so ensure that you don't spill the packets in your food. Place them in the bottom of the container, or buried deep within its contents. Avoid placing them next to an oxygen absorber as it will interfere with its activity.

Storeroom Conditions

To wrap up this chapter, let's focus on your storeroom, which must be kept in good condition. Your storeroom needs to meet a few key criteria for better effectiveness. Remember all the different elements that you need to protect your food from? You must take the time to ensure that your storeroom is suitable for those not accounted for by your packaging.

The best packaging in the world will be useless if you've got a storeroom full of rats who will chew right through it for a quick snack. Likewise, somewhere with constant temperature fluctuations is likely to be problematic. If you want your storeroom to be effective, make sure you implement the following:

- Make sure your storeroom is cool, dry, and well-ventilated.
- Keep the temperature between 50° and 70°F.
- Keep the space free from uninsulated pipes, water heaters, or anything else that may generate heat.
- Keep the humidity level at 15% or less.
- Avoid food being kept in direct sunlight to prevent a reduction in fat-soluble vitamins.
- Store foods at least 6 inches off the floor, and 18 inches from outside walls.

The most important thing that you can do with your stockpile of food is to ensure that it is stored well. It will taste better as a result, and it will also preserve its nutritional value. When your food is stored well, it lasts significantly longer, as you will protect it from light, oxygen, insects, and rodents. By treating your food, storing it in the right containers, and keeping your storeroom in the right condition, you'll find that your food stockpile is kept better.

Chapter Summary

In this chapter, we emphasized the importance of having the right containers and treatment methods to protect your dry goods.

- The most important elements your containers need to protect against are oxygen, light, insects and rodents.
- The most popular storage options are Mylar bags, cans, PET bottles, plastic buckets, and glass jars.
- By treating with dry ice, oxygen absorbers, diatomaceous earth, or silica gel, the shelf life of foods can be extended.
- Keeping your storeroom in excellent condition is essential to ensuring that your food is kept safe.

6

CANNING 101: THE BASICS OF PRESERVING FRESH INGREDIENTS FOR MAXIMUM NUTRITIONAL VALUE

So far, we've spent a lot of time talking about dried goods, but those will only go so far, especially if you're interested in keeping fresh vegetables from your garden. This is where canning comes into play. While tins can keep dry foods long-term, you can also use canning jars if you want to preserve your produce to last in the middle of winter. With canning, you can preserve that delicious tomato sauce you made with freshly picked tomatoes, or the nutritious soup you made from scratch. Having some fruits and vegetables on hand is a great way to stretch your harvest so you're feeding yourself all year-round instead of just during the summer months.

Canning is a great way to preserve produce without damaging its nutritional content. When you choose to can your food, you usually have two options: canning with boiling water baths or canning with pressure canning. Most will be canned with pressure, but when you have high-acid foods, such as an abundance of tomatoes from your garden, you can use the boiling water bath option instead.

It might seem intimidating, but it is how people stored their food for generations before the popularization of grocery stores. You've probably heard horror stories about food poisoning, botulism, spoilage, and pressure canners blowing up, but keep in mind that if you do things just right, you'll be just fine.

You can grow your food during the summer, and then enjoy working on storing it as it's harvested. By reading this chapter, you'll discover what you need to know about canning to make sure you're doing it safely. We'll begin by discussing the vegetables that don't usually can very well, followed by how canning works. We'll go over the tools and then the process itself. We'll break it down into a few simple steps: sterilizing jars, filling jars, and then canning. We will discuss both the boiling water bath and the pressure canning methods. Finally, we'll go over the processing time for the most common produce people tend to can.

VEGETABLES THAT DON'T CAN WELL

Some produce simply doesn't can well. It may pose a risk to your health if you can it, or it may taste so bad you won't want to bother. Many of these items fare much better if you freeze them instead.

Broccoli

Broccoli isn't necessarily dangerous to can, but it won't taste very good when you open it up. It will be so mushy and soft that it won't be enjoyable. It's usually better to pickle it if you want to store it, or you can choose to freeze your broccoli instead.

Brussels Sprouts

Brussels sprouts are unappealing when canned as they get slimy and lose their flavor. They usually do well when they're pickled, however, so they can still be preserved.

Cabbage

Cabbage will be safe to eat after pressure canning it, but it will be slimy, mushy and unenjoyable. However, pickling it is a good option.

Cauliflower

Like broccoli, cauliflower will not be harmful to eat, but it won't be enjoyable when it's been canned. Pressure canning is likely to create something mushy and unpleasant to eat.

Celery

Celery does not currently have an approved method of canning. Some people will attempt it anyway, but it's not been safety-tested, so there are no safe processing times currently determined. If you want to save celery, freeze it instead.

Eggplant

Eggplant will become mushy and ultimately disgusting if you use a pressure canner. However, you can pickle it if you want to.

Kohlrabi

Canned kohlrabi usually has unpleasant and overly soft results. It's better to pickle this vegetable instead of trying to save it. You can choose to freeze it instead.

Lettuce

Like cabbage, lettuce will become slimy and inedible if it is canned. Lettuce is not heated to eat, and it also doesn't freeze well. There is no good way to store it long-term. Stick to enjoying your lettuce fresh.

Zucchini

There has not yet been any research into how to can zucchini properly. Because squash, like zucchini, is a little bit acidic, it is at risk of developing botulism in low-oxygen environments, and currently, it is unknown how long zucchini should be processed in a pressure canner. Rather than pressure canning it, consider pickling it or freezing it instead.

HOW CANNING WORKS

Canning, despite sounding intimidating, is simple. It works by putting foods in jars or other similar, heat-tolerant containers such as cans, and heating them to temperatures that will destroy all the potential microorganisms that may have been present in the food to cause it to spoil. As the jar is heated, the air is forced out from the jar, and when it cools off again, a vacuum seal is created. This vacuum seal then prevents any air from re-entering the jar, which locks out any microorganisms that could have contaminated it.

Usually, the jar is heated in one of two ways. You can use a boiling-water bath, which is usually recommended for fruits, tomatoes, jellies and jams, pickles, and other pickled goods. In the bath, jars are heated by covering them completely with boiling water to cook for a specified amount of time. I've included a handy chart at the end of this chapter for you to use as a reference to see how long each food you'd like to can will need to be warmed.

You can also use pressure canning, which is currently the only safe method you can use to preserve vegetables, meats, seafood, or poultry. During pressure canning, the jars are placed in a few inches of water within a pressure cooker, which is then heated to at least 240°F. This is achieved through pressurizing the environment. This method is necessary because of clostridium botulinum. This is the organism responsible for botulism. Though the cells can be killed at boiling temperatures, the spores they create can still survive. The spores can grow rapidly in low-acid foods, which meats and veggies are classed as. As the spores grow, they then release toxins that can be deadly. These spores are only killed off when you pressure-cook food at a temperature of 240°F or higher for a specific amount of time, depending upon the type of food and your altitude.

High-acid foods can usually kill the spores without allowing for the release of the toxins, but to reach that acidity, the food would need to have a pH of 4.6 or lower. This is typically applicable to fruits or pickled vegetables which are canned in brine or vinegar. Some foods, like tomatoes, are close to this pH value, so they are usually canned with the addition of some lemon juice or citric acid.

WHAT YOU NEED FOR CANNING

Food safety is no joke, and it's so easy to unintentionally set up an environment to become infected with botulism. You need to make sure you have the right tools on hand. While it's highly unlikely that, even if you can something poorly, it will develop botulism, the risk is there, and it's always better to be safe than sorry, especially where your family's wellbeing is concerned. The best thing you can do when it comes to canning is to ensure that you gather all the right tools to help protect the foods.

Canning Jars and Lids

Canning jars come in several shapes and sizes, with many different lids. Ultimately, the ones you choose are up to you. So long as they are glass and well-made, they're good enough to use. Just make sure that none of them are damaged before you get started.

You'll also want to make sure that you have the right lids. Some jars are reusable, but others must be replaced each time you use them. Verify which kind you have, and when in doubt, always opt for new lids if you're unsure. Select jars in various sizes so you can store everything from jams to sauces and larger quantities of veggies or pickles. Lids may be one-piece or two-piece, so long as you verify that they're the right size.

Tongs or Jar Remover

Tongs may work just fine for removing jars, but you run the risk dropping them, which could be dangerous at such high temperatures. It's recommended that you get a jar remover, which has rubber grips that won't conduct heat, and will grip the top of your jar tightly as you remove it from the water bath.

Funnel

A canning funnel is specifically designed to fit into jars to allow you to keep your rims cleaner, which is necessary in order to get a proper seal. They also allow you to get everything into the jar easily, since you'll be able to use the funnel to guide everything in. Choose one specifically designed for filling jars for the best results.

A Pressure Canner

Canning can be done in just about any large pot, but if you're going to pressure can, you'll need something that will create the necessary pressure. A pressure canner will trap the steam within it to pressurize the container and raise the temperature further.

THE CANNING PROCESS

Sterilizing Jars

The first step of canning is to begin the process with sterile jars. This is essential. While the process of canning will raise the temperature to kill bacteria, it's still good to make sure you're working with as clean an environment as possible: If you're off with your temperatures even a little, you'll be risking a lot. The sterilization process is, thankfully, quite easy.

- **Discard damaged jars.** Start by going through all the jars you intend to use and inspecting them carefully. Any cracks or nicks in the jar's rim can interfere with the vacuum seal you're trying to achieve. If you notice any jars that are damaged, discard them. They're not safe to use.
- **Sanitize jars and lids.** When you know which cans you'll be using, wash them in hot water with soap, and dry them completely. Alternatively, you can run them through the dishwasher to sanitize them and get them ready to go.
- **Keep jars warm.** Once they've been sanitized,

set your jars in the oven, set at 180°F. This is an essential step: You don't want to put hot food into a cold jar, or a cold jar into a boiling hot bath. By keeping them hot, you can prevent this from happening.

Filling Jars

With the jars prepared and ready to fill, it's time to load them up. Keep in mind that all the jars are still hot, so do not handle them bare-handed. Instead, use a jar lifter or oven mitts to protect yourself. With that in mind, take the following steps to fill the jars:

- **Fill Jars:** Using your funnel, pour food or liquid into the jars. Each recipe you choose to jar will have a different allowance for headspace, which will vary by ingredients. Follow this recommendation. The headspace is the space in the jar between the food and the top of the jar.
- **Remove Air Bubbles:** When the jars are full, use something long and skinny, like a wooden skewer or rubber spatula, to dislodge any air bubbles. There are bubble remover tools, but these are rarely necessary.
- **Wipe Rims:** When all the jars are filled, make sure the rims are clean to prevent anything from impeding a vacuum seal. Now's not the

time to be messy: You want everything as immaculate as possible. You can use a clean, damp cloth for this process. Just make sure there's no lint left behind.

- **Tighten Lids:** Place the lids on the jars and tighten them. If you're using two-piece jar lids, make sure you center the flat part and then tighten the band until it is finger-tight. Your jars are now ready for processing.

Boiling Water Bath

The boiling water bath method is quite easy. When your jars are ready to be processed, you can simply move on. Remember that you should only use the boiling water bath if you're canning something high in acid. This can't be reiterated enough. Any low-acid foods should *never* be processed in this manner. It's repeated as often as it is for a reason: Botulism is fatal, sometimes up to 50% of the time, if you cannot seek medical treatment. Don't risk it. Properly can your food.

High-acid foods can be stored for between 12 and 18 months in this manner, so if you want to preserve your fruits or acidic vegetables using this method, continue with the rest of these instructions. Otherwise, skip to the next section to learn how to pressure can.

How to Boil Jars

When it's time to boil your jars, there are a few simple steps, and the only extra equipment you'll need is a container that is deep enough to allow for the jars to be submerged, and something that will lift the jars off the bottom of the pot to allow for full circulation of the water as they are boiled. There are many jar-lifters you can get for this process.

1. Make sure that your jars have been sterilized before you begin the canning process. Once you have sterilized jars, place them in a large pot and fill the pot with water. The water needs to be able to cover the jars. Begin to simmer the water at 180°F for 10 minutes. This is done to prevent the jars from breaking when they are filled with hot food (this process is called hot packing) or when the jars are placed in the boiling water bath. It is important to keep the jars in the simmering water until they are ready to be hot-packed.

2. Using a funnel, fill the food into the hot jars. Refer to the recipe or table you are using to gauge the required headspace (the empty space that needs to be left between the food and the lid). It is important to remove any air bubbles that may have been created, so taking a non-

metal tool like a spatula or a plastic chopstick, carefully work the tool down the jars and remove any air bubbles. You might need to put more food into the jar to maintain the headspace once the air bubbles have been removed.

3. Clean off any leftover sauce on the jar rims. This can be done with a cloth or damp paper towel. This will ensure the jars are sealed properly.

4. Next, place the bands and lids on the jars. Tighten the bands until you feel slight resistance. Make sure not to overtighten the jars. It will not make the jars seal better in fact you will achieve the opposite. Always use new lids. You can reuse bands if they are in good condition

5. Fill the canner halfway with boiling water. Bring the water to a full simmer. Gently lower the jars one at a time into the water with a jar lifter. You can use a canning rack to lower all the jars at once, but being gentle is the key. Pay close attention to the water level. If the water level does not cover the jars by 1 to 2 inches, you will need to add more boiling water until the water covers the jars. Bring the water to a

rolling boil, cover the canner and boil for as
long as the recipe requires.

6. Once the time is up, turn off the heat, remove
the lid and let the water in the canner cool for
10 minutes before you take the jars out.

7. Use the jar lifter to remove the jars and let them
cool. Keeping them upright on a towel, wire
rack, or cutting board, keep them roughly 1 to 2
inches apart. Do not retighten the rims even if
you hear a pinging noise. This is just the jars
cooling and sealing. Leave the jars in their new
position without any disturbances for 12-24
hours.

8. Checking the seals is an exciting and important
part of the canning process. Simply push the
center of the lid down. You are looking for the
center of the lid to remain down and not pop
up. To double-check the seal, remove the band
and try to remove the lid. If the lid does not
move, you have a good seal. Sadly, if the center
does pop up or you are able to remove the lid
easily, the jar is not sealed. In this case, store the
food in the fridge for up to 3 weeks or in the
freezer for up to 1 year.

9. Label all jars and store them in a cool, dark, and
dry place, so they are ready to enjoy!

Pressure Canning

For your low-acid foods, pressure canning will keep them safe. This is also effective if you want to can complete meals, like soups, stews and sauces. You can even preserve meats in this fashion if you want something shelf-stable. This process will require you to get a pressure canner.

How to Pressure Can

This process is a bit more involved than using a water bath, but it can be just as effective. You will want to follow these steps:

1. Begin with sterilized jars and lids. Then place a rack in the bottom of your pressure canner.

Add boiling water to it. Usually, you want to have about 3 inches of water at the bottom of the canner.

2. Place your filled jars into the canner, not touching anywhere, then attach the lid. Allow the steam to leave the petcock opening for 10 minutes, then shut it until the steam comes out in a steady stream.

3. Turn the heat off, and leave the whole thing alone until the pressure has reached 0 and stays there for a few minutes. Then, you can remove the lid and start pulling out the jars with the jar lifter. Leave them to cool completely on a dry tea towel.

Processing Time

Boiling Method (Acidic Foods)

Headspace: On all high acid foods listed in the tables below leave 1/2 inch headspace. With the exception of strawberry jam which needs 1/4 inch and grapes which need 1 inch headspace.

FOOD TYPE	PACK METHOD	PROCESS TIME (PINT)	PROCESS TIME (QUART)
APPLES	HOT	20 MINS	20 MINS
APRICOTS	RAW; HOT	25 MINS; 20 MINS	30 MINS; 25 MINS
BLACKBERRIES	RAW; HOT	15 MINS; 15 MINS	20 MINS; 15 MINS
BLUEBERRIES	RAW; HOT	15 MINS; 15 MINS	20 MINS; 15 MINS
CRANBERRIES	HOT	15 MINS	15 MINS
CHERRIES	RAW; HOT	25 MINS; 15 MINS	30 MINS; 20 MINS
CUCUMBERS (PICKLED)	RAW	10 MINS	15 MINS
GRAPEFRUIT	RAW	10 MINS	15 MINS
GRAPES	RAW; HOT	15 MINS; 10 MINS	20 MINS; 10 MINS

FOOD TYPE	PACK METHOD	PROCESS TIME (PINT)	PROCESS TIME (QUART)
NECTARINES	RAW; HOT	25 MINS; 20 MINS	30 MINS; 25 MINS
ORANGES	RAW	10 MINS	10 MINS
PEACHES	RAW; HOT	25 MINS; 20 MINS	30 MINS; 25 MINS
PEARS	RAW; HOT	25 MINS; 20 MINS	30 MINS; 25 MINS
PINEAPPLE	HOT	15 MINS	20 MINS
PLUMS	RAW; HOT	20 MINS; 25 MINS	20 MINS; 25 MINS
RASPBERRIES	RAW; HOT	15 MINS; 15 MINS	20 MINS; 15 MINS
RHUBARB	HOT	15 MINS	15 MINS
STRAWBERRY JAM	HOT	5 MINS	15 MINS

FOOD TYPE	PACK METHOD	PROCESS TIME (PINT)	PROCESS TIME (QUART)
TOMATO JUICE	HOT	35 MINS	40 MINS
TOMATOES (WHOLE, HALVED)	RAW	85 MINS	85 MINS
TOMATOES (CRUSHED)	HOT	35 MINS	40 MINS

THE PROCESSING TIMES FOR THE COMPLETE TABLES ABOVE ARE FOR CANNING AT SEA LEVEL. MODIFY AS SHOWN IN THE TABLE BELOW:	
PROCESSING TIME AT SEA LEVEL	MODIFIED PROCESSING TIME
20 MINUTES OR LESS	ADD 1 MINUTE PER 1000 FT. IN ELEVATION
OVER 20 MINUTES	ADD 2 MINUTES PER 1000 FT. IN ELEVATION

Pressure Canning (Acidic Foods)

Headspace: On all high acidic foods listed below leave 1/2 inch headspace. For each 1000 feet above sea level increase the headspace by 1/8 inch. For pint jars do not exceed 1 inch headspace and on quart jars 1 3/4 inch headspace.

FOOD TYPE	PACK METHOD	PROCESS TIME PINT	PROCESS TIME QUART	PSI UNDER 2,000 FT.	PSI 2,001-4,000 FT.	PSI 4,001-6,000 FT.	PSI 6,001-8,000 FT.
APPLES	HOT	8 MINS	8 MINS	6 LB	7 LB	8 LB	9 LB
APRICOTS	RAW; HOT	10 MINS; 10 MINS	10 MINS; 10 MINS	6 LB; 6 LB	7 LB; 7 LB	8 LB; 8 LB	9 LB; 9 LB
BLACKBERRIES	RAW; HOT	8 MINS; 8 MINS	10 MINS; 8 MINS	6 LB; 6 LB	7 LB; 7 LB	8 LB; 8 LB	9 LB; 9 LB
BLUEBERRIES	RAW; HOT	8 MINS; 8 MINS	10 MINS; 8 MINS	6 LB; 6 LB	7 LB; 7 LB	8 LB; 8 LB	9 LB; 9 LB
CHERRIES	RAW; HOT	10 MINS; 8 MINS	10 MINS; 10 MINS	6 LB; 6 LB	7 LB; 7 LB	8 LB; 8 LB	9 LB; 9 LB
GRAPEFRUIT	RAW; HOT	8 MINS; 10 MINS	10 MINS; 10 MINS	6 LB; 6 LB	7 LB; 7 LB	8 LB; 8 LB	9 LB; 9 LB
NECTARINES	RAW; HOT	10 MINS; 10 MINS	10 MINS; 10 MINS	6 LB; 6 LB	7 LB; 7 LB	8 LB; 8 LB	9 LB; 9 LB
ORANGES	RAW; HOT	8 MINS; 10 MINS	10 MINS; 10 MINS	6 LB; 6 LB	7 LB; 7 LB	8 LB; 8 LB	9 LB; 9 LB
PEACHES	RAW; HOT	10 MINS; 10 MINS	10 MINS; 10 MINS	6 LB; 6 LB	7 LB; 7 LB	8 LB; 8 LB	9 LB; 9 LB
PEARS	HOT	10 MINS	10 MINS	6 LB	7 LB	8 LB	9 LB

FOOD TYPE	PACK METHOD	PROCESS TIME PINT	PROCESS TIME QUART	PSI UNDER 2,000 FT.	PSI 2,001-4,000 FT.	PSI 4,001-6,000 FT.	PSI 6,001-8,000 FT.
PLUMS	RAW; HOT	10 MINS; 10 MINS	10 MINS; 10 MINS	6 LB; 6 LB	7 LB; 7 LB	8 LB; 8 LB	9 LB; 9 LB
RASPBERRIES	RAW; HOT	8 MINS; 10 MINS	10 MINS; 8 MINS	6 LB; 6 LB	7 LB; 7 LB	8 LB; 8 LB	9 LB; 9 LB
RHUBARB	HOT	8 MINS	8 MINS	6 LB	7 LB	8 LB	9 LB
TOMATO JUICE	HOT	20 MINS	20 MINS	6 LB	7 LB	8 LB	9 LB
TOMATOES (WHOLE, HALVED)	RAW	40 MINS	40 MINS	6 LB	7 LB	8 LB	9 LB
TOMATOES (CRUSHED)	HOT	20 MINS	20 MINS	6 LB	7 LB	8 LB	9 LB

Pressure Canning (Low Acid Foods)

Headspace: On all low acid foods listed below leave 1 inch headspace. Except lima beans, raw packed in quart size jars, increase headspace to 1 1/2 inch for small beans and for large beans 1 1/4 inch. For each 1000 feet above sea level increase the headspace by 1/8 inch. For pint jars do not exceed 1 inch headspace and on quart jars 1 3/4 inch headspace.

FOOD TYPE	PACK METHOD	PROCESS TIME PINT	PROCESS TIME QUART	PSI UNDER 2,000 FT.	PSI 2,001-4,000 FT.	PSI 4,001-6,000 FT.	PSI 6,001-8,000 FT.
ARTICHOKES (JERUSALEM)	HOT	25 MINS	25 MINS	11 LB	12 LB	13 LB	14 LB
ASPARAGUS	RAW; HOT	30 MINS; 30 MINS	40 MINS; 40 MINS	11 LB; 11 LB	12 LB; 12 LB	13 LB; 13 LB	14 LB; 14 LB
BEANS (GREEN OR YELLOW)	RAW; HOT	20 MINS; 20 MINS	25 MINS; 25 MINS	11 LB; 11 LB	12 LB; 12 LB	13 LB; 13 LB	14 LB; 14 LB
BEETS	HOT	30 MINS	35 MINS	11 LB	12 LB	13 LB	14 LB
CARROTS	RAW; HOT	25 MINS; 25 MINS	30 MINS; 30 MINS	11 LB; 11 LB	12 LB; 12 LB	13 LB; 13 LB	14 LB; 14 LB
CORN	RAW; HOT	55 MINS; 55 MINS	85 MINS; 85 MINS	11 LB; 11 LB	12 LB; 12 LB	13 LB; 13 LB	14 LB; 14 LB
LIMA BEANS	RAW; HOT	40 MINS; 40 MINS	50 MINS; 50 MINS	11 LB; 11 LB	12 LB; 12 LB	13 LB; 13 LB	14 LB; 14 LB
MUSHROOMS	HOT	45 MINS	---	11 LB	12 LB	13 LB	14 LB
OKRA	RAW; HOT	25 MINS; 25 MINS	40 MINS; 40 MINS	11 LB; 11 LB	12 LB; 12 LB	13 LB; 13 LB	14 LB; 14 LB
PEAS	RAW; HOT	40 MINS; 40 MINS	40 MINS; 40 MINS	11 LB; 11 LB	12 LB; 12 LB	13 LB; 13 LB	14 LB; 14 LB
PEPPERS	HOT	35 MINS	---	11 LB	12 LB	13 LB	14 LB

FOOD TYPE	PACK METHOD	PROCESS TIME PINT	PROCESS TIME QUART	PSI UNDER 2,000 FT.	PSI 2,001-4,000 FT.	PSI 4,001-6,000 FT.	PSI 6,001-8,000 FT.
POTATOES (WHITE)	HOT	35 MINS	40 MINS	11 LB	12 LB	13 LB	14 LB
PUMPKIN	HOT	55 MINS	90 MINS	11 LB	12 LB	13 LB	14 LB
SPINACH AND LEAFY GREENS	HOT	70 MINS	90 MINS	11 LB	12 LB	13 LB	14 LB
WINTER SQUASH	HOT	55 MINS	90 MINS	11 LB	12 LB	13 LB	14 LB
SWEET POTATOES	HOT	65 MINS	90 MINS	11 LB	12 LB	13 LB	14 LB

Canning foods is a great way for you to keep them for longer than they'd otherwise last in the fridge or on a shelf. However, it can also cause changes to the texture of your food. As you know by now, certain foods simply don't can well, but they can be pickled. When you can your food, you must make sure that you do so in the right way. While all foods can be pressure canned, not all canning-friendly foods can be canned with a bath. Remember that because of the risk of botulism, foods should always be canned according to the recommendations for those foods.

Chapter Summary

In this chapter, we have reviewed how to can fresh foods so they can be kept on a shelf. We covered:

- What canning will do and how it keeps your food safe.
- Which foods shouldn't be canned.
- What you need in order to can your food.
- How to sterilize and fill jars.
- How to use a boiling water bath.
- How to use a pressure canner.
- Why it's so important to pressure can low-acid foods.
- The processing times for varying foods.

7

THE CHEST FREEZER: WHY YOU NEED ONE NOW, AND WHAT YOU NEED TO FILL IT WITH

Y our stockpile isn't complete without a chest freezer that's been loaded up with fresh ingredients to thaw and use later. Most emergencies aren't likely to completely disrupt your ability to access power, so it's always a good idea to keep frozen food on hand. Plus, you can usually take advantage of some great shopping deals when you have a chest freezer, whether that's through catching meat on sale at a great price or taking advantage of the hunting season.

A chest freezer will provide you with extra space. For many people, the freezer attached to their refrigerator is a great start, but there's a good chance that you can't keep much more than a few days' worth of meat in there, especially if you're already keeping frozen snacks, convenience meals, and ice cream in there. A deep freezer can become a sort of reserve area where you can store meat for longer periods. They're also good for storing bread, vegetables, fruits for smoothies, eggs, and prepared foods that are quick and easy to heat.

This is likely to be your first line of defense if you can't easily get to the grocery store, as the food usually tastes better than canned food, it's more nutritious, and it's likely to be closer to what you normally eat. However, it's a good idea to make sure you don't only stock up in this manner, as if something happens to the power, you'll lose everything in a few days.

If you want to be on the safe side, you should consider an alternative source of electricity in case the grid were to go down for an extended period of time.

As you read through this chapter, we'll go over why a chest freezer is better than an upright model. We'll discuss the benefits of freezing foods and why it's so widely recommended. We'll discuss what to prioritize when your freezer space is limited, and what should be left out of the freezer entirely. We'll also go over some simple tips that you can use to ensure that you're able to maximize the use of your freezer and keep your family fed and happy, even in an emergency.

WHY CHOOSE A CHEST FREEZER?

Chest freezers aren't always the most popular choice. They have a much larger footprint than an upright freezer, and it's often harder to dig through them to find what you're looking for just because many food-stuffs will wind up buried as you fill up the freezer. You can only see what's on the top layer, which, while inconvenient, can be a good thing, as we'll be discussing.

While a chest freezer is undoubtedly less convenient, it's the better option if you're choosing to stockpile food, and there are several reasons for this. If you have the option, it's always better for you to select a chest freezer over other models.

More Usable Space

Chest freezers may not be fun to dig through, but you can benefit from more usable space. There is roughly 20% more usable space in a chest freezer than in a similarly-sized upright freezer. That increase in usable space means 20% more food you can stash away for when you need it.

More Consistent Temperature

Chest freezers keep a more consistent temperature than upright models. This is because they don't come with a self-defrost system. This is good for your food: It's more likely to stay safely frozen rather than thawing out. However, it may need to be defrosted now and then when frost has accumulated.

Less Air Circulation

Chest freezers don't have as much space for air circulation. This is a great thing for the long-term storage of food: Your food is going to be well-protected from freezer burn.

Keeps Food Frozen Longer

If there is a blackout or something that causes you to lose all power for an extended period, a chest freezer will keep your food frozen for longer just because you can fill up so much more space. The proximity of other frozen items will help each one stay frozen for longer.

Uses Less Electricity

Most chest freezers use up less electricity than uprights, but you'll have to compare while you're shopping to make sure you select the most energy-efficient option.

WHY FREEZE YOUR FOOD

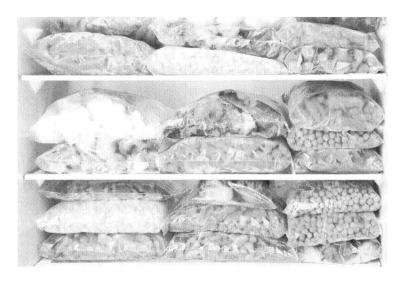

You might wonder if there are any inherent benefits to freezing your food, and in fact, there are many. Freezing food is a fantastic way to save on food, and many people who garden and hunt go out of their way to have several chest freezers on hand so that they're able to keep all of their bounties from going bad.

Freezing your food is highly effective for keeping it safe. If you keep the temperature at a constant 32°F, then the food is going to be safe, whether it's one year or four years old. Will it taste as good? Probably not. Usually, long-term storage can affect the taste a little.

Ideally, you want to get a good deep freezer; the lower the temperature you can get from your freezer, the better. Typically, the foods at the bottom of your freezer will fare better than the foods at the top, where they may be exposed to regular temperatures during the day.

By freezing food, you'll get the added benefit of enjoying fresh meat, fish, bread, and other complete meals that have already been prepared. This allows for better nutrition and variety, and you can even tailor your meals to what you want to eat each day. If you're sick, you could prioritize pulling out the ingredients to make a fresh, nutritious soup, for example. This isn't possible with canned foods. You'll also get better taste and texture out of your frozen food as it wasn't cooked during the canning process and then left to sit in its moisture for an extended amount of time. It will taste truer to its original state, especially if you can keep the food minimally processed and well frozen.

WHAT TO PRIORITIZE WHEN FREEZER SPACE IS LIMITED

When you've got limited space in your freezer, it's tough to figure out which foods you want to store. However, some foods are better to keep than others. Generally, you'll want to keep foods that don't take up as much space. You may even want to make it a point to break down certain items so they fit better in the limited space you have. For example, imagine you have a whole chicken you just bought from the store. It's going to take up a lot more space than if you take the time to spatchcock it or to butcher it entirely.

You want to prioritize proteins like meat, poultry, and fish. These are usually better frozen than canned, but you can them if you'd like to. Then, prioritize any fruits and vegetables that don't suit the canning process. From there, you can add additional vegetables and fruits if you prefer them to be in a whole or frozen state. They could be great for smoothies. If you've already stocked up on these, you can store breads, baked goods, and leftovers from meals. Just keep in mind that some things may change in flavor or texture during the freezing process.

What Not to Freeze

Just as some foods aren't suitable for canning, several foods may not do so well frozen. Generally, the more processed something is, the worse it will fare in freezing. You want to avoid freezing products such as:

- Bacon
- Canned meats or fish
- Cream cheese
- Deli meats and cheeses
- Eggplant

- Melon
- Raw potatoes
- Radishes
- Salads and lettuce
- Sprouts
- Whole eggs (they may freeze decently if cracked and stored, or if you scramble and cook them first, but there will be a change in texture)

FREEZING TIPS

When freezing food for storage, there are ways you can help extend the time that it will remain undamaged by freezer burn. There are also ways that you can keep track of your stash better, so you always know exactly what you have available to you. By following the tips and tricks provided here, you can protect your food from freezer burn, fit more into your storage, and ensure that, in the event of a power outage, your food will remain safe in the time before the power comes back on.

Leave No Space Unfilled

By filling every space of your freezer, you can achieve two goals. First, it is harder for your freezer to warm up when there is more in there, meaning that in the event of a power outage, the food won't thaw out as quickly.

The food in the freezer will act like ice packs to help insulate all the other food in there. Second, by filling every space efficiently, you can fit more into your freezer, extending your stash and ensuring that you'll have more available to you when you need it.

If there are sizeable gaps in your freezer and you're not quite ready to fill them in with food, consider adding in jugs or bags full of water. These will fill in space to protect your food, and you can simply pull them out when it's time to put more food in its place.

However, keep in mind that you shouldn't pack food too tightly either, as water expands when it freezes. To prevent damage to the food or the storage bags, keeping the right amount of food is essential.

Cool Completely before Freezing

While it might seem like common sense to cool food before putting it into a freezer, this is something that some people will forego, especially if they're trying to put away precooked meals. However, by putting in foods that aren't already cooled, you are causing the freezer's temperature to rise. It may not be enough to thaw out your food, but it is a health hazard. You can thaw and refreeze certain foods without realizing it, which can dramatically reduce the shelf-life of the food. Always make sure that food is at least at room temperature, but preferably cooler, before putting it into your freezer.

Label and Date Everything

When you don't label your foods, you may thaw something entirely different from what you were expecting. That frozen beef stew? It might end up being soup or a sauce from a pre-made meal. A chunk of what you think is ham may end up being some pork loin. By labeling everything, you will know exactly what's in each bag: no surprises. If applicable, the label should also include preparation instructions.

Dating everything is essential as well. While, technically, food may remain safe indefinitely when you leave it in a freezer, it will not remain tasty indefinitely. It will lose quality over time, so you will want to use older foods first. This means you need a dating system so you can compare which food is newer before selecting it.

Seal Properly

Before putting any food into the freezer, a proper seal is essential if you want to extend the longevity of the food. You don't want frost to enter and change the taste of the foods.

Use a Vacuum Sealer for Long-Term Storage

This brings us to our next tip: using vacuum sealers for long-term storage. These can be incredibly handy items, whether you're saving dry goods or foods to put in the freezer. A vacuum sealer is relatively inexpensive and you can use it to ensure that all the air has been pulled out of the storage bag. By getting that perfect seal with no air coming through, the food is protected better and for longer. You can extend how long food lasts in the freezer once it's been vacuum-sealed.

Keep the Freezer Frost-Free

Freezers shouldn't be full of frost when you open them up. Identifying frost in the freezer is a sign that moisture is coming into contact with coils. This can cause problems with odors, storage space being taken up by frost, and even difficulty with shutting the door. Frost may also cause freezer burn on food as moisture evaporates and freezes, ruining the taste of the food.

Freeze in Portion Sizes

If you've got a massive amount of meat or pre-made meals to freeze, it's always a good idea to freeze them in portion sizes for individuals or the entire family. This way, you are only ever defrosting what you need, rather than having to pull out an entire roasting joint when you only need half to feed everyone. Portion sizes are also a little easier to puzzle-piece together when necessary to maximize space in your freezer.

Keep Long-Term Storage on the Bottom

This may be a bit of common sense, but if you have things you're keeping long-term for any reason, these foods should go to the bottom of the freezer. The bottom is the coldest part, which means the food will keep longer, but you're also not having to dig past it constantly to access other items that you have in there.

Freezers are vital tools, but they should always be used in tandem with other methods of storing your food. This means that if you're going to keep food in a freezer to reap the higher nutritional benefits this method of storage offers, you should have plenty of canned or shelf-stable options as well. Remember that you could lose power, or your freezer could die on you. It may not happen, but it's always better to be prepared. Keep your freezer stocked with meat, fish, poultry, vegetables, and fruits, and if you have room, toss in some pre-made meals for easy access.

Chapter Summary

In this chapter, we discussed the importance of freezing food for emergency scenarios. The key points to remember are:

- Chest freezers are better than standing freezers.
- When you have limited freezer space, prioritize meat, poultry, fish, vegetables, and fruits.
- Food can be frozen indefinitely if it remains frozen, but it will lose flavor and nutrients.
- A freezer is a valuable tool, but it should not be your only line of defense.

8

DEHYDRATING 101: EVERYTHING YOU NEED TO KNOW TO PRESERVE NUTRITIONAL CONTENT THROUGH DEHYDRATION

If you're looking for ways to store food that are not dependent on refrigeration, dehydration is a great way to do so. Dehydrated foods pack all the nutritional punch of fresh foods, without the space commitment and stringent storage parameters. Dehydrated foods that were nutritious while fresh will also be nutritious when dried. All you have to do is add some water and you'll have a meal, or at least a component of one.

In this chapter, we will discuss what dehydration is and the benefits it offers. We'll discuss the most common methods of dehydration, as well as what should not be dehydrated. Then we'll take the time to go over how to dehydrate several foods. Finally, we'll wrap it up by discussing how to rehydrate food.

Dehydration provides you with the ability to preserve the nutritional value of produce by removing all water from the food. With little moisture in the food, you'll be able to then extend the lifespan of it. Without moisture, it's difficult for most bacteria to grow on it, even if the food is not refrigerated. Dehydrated foods may remain fresh for 5–15 years.

METHODS OF DEHYDRATION

Dehydration can be achieved in several ways: air drying, sun drying, oven drying, through food dehydrators, or even in smokehouses. The method you choose is entirely based upon resources available to you, as well as your preference.

Air Drying

Air drying involves hanging foods indoors to dry in the air. There must be good airflow for this, and foods must be protected from dirt and insects. Keep in mind that this only really works in low-humidity areas, or the food may develop mold before it dries.

Sun Drying

Sun drying is the oldest method of drying. It is entirely free if you live somewhere with plenty of sun. However, because it requires the weather to be onside, it cannot be planned for accurately. Food will usually take three or four days to dry in the sun, and if it doesn't dry in that period, it's likely to develop mold. Ideally, the sky should be clear and the temperature should be 95ºF or higher for three to five days, along with less than 20% humidity. If you can't guarantee all these conditions, this method is not for you.

Oven Drying

The oven can dry food easily. It may take six or more hours to dry food properly. These foods will require low heat, and some may only require a gas pilot light to dry effectively. You should set your oven to 140ºF if possible, leaving the door ajar to allow for circulation. However, this is a very expensive method due to how long it will take. You may also accidentally burn food.

FOOD DEHYDRATORS

Food dehydrators contain some sort of heating element, alongside fans and vents to heat the air and circulate it to dry out foods. Dried foods will shrink and become lighter, and with a good dehydrator, more flavor and color are kept. These usually allow for more food to be dried faster, consistently, and sometimes more energy efficiently. However, these devices take up counter space, and they can be expensive if you choose one with all the bells and whistles.

Smokehouse Drying

Foods, especially meats, can be dried in a smoker. This will not only dry out the food, but it will add a nice smoky flavor as well. This usually requires a temperature of 145°–150ºF, with plenty of smoke to dry the food out. This can take between 12 and 72 hours, depending on the food.

What Not to Dehydrate

Some foods that may be available commercially in dried forms are not safe to dry at home for safety reasons. In particular, you want to avoid dehydrating butter, cheese, eggs, or milk. It's too easy to do so poorly or cause spoilage. However, dried eggs, cheese, butter, and milk should definitely be purchased as part of your stockpile.

PREPARING FOODS FOR DEHYDRATION

The best foods to dehydrate are those that will hold their nutritional value easily. Leafy greens, many forms of produce, and some meats can be dehydrated easily for simple snacks. However, before dehydrating, certain foods must be treated first.

Blanching before Dehydration

Certain foods must be blanched before being dehydrated. This is cooking food in steam or water for a specific amount of time, and then cooling it quickly. Blanching works well for asparagus, carrots, peas, tomatoes, cranberries, cherries, onions, blueberries, plums, pears, potatoes, pumpkin, turnips, wax or green beans, and rutabagas. To blanch, you will need a stockpot of boiling water, a bowl of icy water, and a slotted spoon. Simply follow these steps:

1. Bring the water in the stockpot to a boil.
2. Add vegetables to create an even layer on top of the water. Put on the lid and let them cook according to the instructions for the food you're dehydrating.
3. After the time has elapsed, remove the food with a slotted spoon and place it in the ice bath to cool.
4. Once it's cool, drain the food and let it dry. Pat

it dry if necessary. It should then be ready to dehydrate.

Boiling Before Dehydration

Certain foods benefit from a quick boil to soften them up before being dehydrated. The most common include butternut squash, beets, potatoes, corn, rhubarb, and beans.

Preparing Meat for Dehydration

Before you dehydrate meat, you must cook it. The cooking method that you choose to use is up to you.

Preparing Fruits for Dehydration

Many fruits will require a dip in citric acid or lemon juice to prevent oxidation, which will cause nutrient loss. Certain fruits, such as bananas, apples, pears, and light-colored stone fruits benefit from this treatment. To do so, you will need citric acid (lemon juice works well), a big bowl or clean sink, and a slotted spoon.

1. Prepare the pre-treatment solution. Citric acid will provide instructions for the particular concentration you need. If you use lemon juice, use one cup of juice for every quart of water, and mix it well.

2. Soak food for up to 10 minutes with lemon juice, or as directed with citric acid.

3. Remove all fruits with the slotted spoon, letting them drain. Dry with a paper towel if possible. The fruits are now ready to be dehydrated.

DEHYDRATING USING A DEHYDRATOR

What You Need

- Dehydrator
- Parchment paper
- Instructions for the ingredient (easily found online)
- Citric acid (prevents oxidation and browning of fruits)
- Storage containers (Mylar bags work well)

Instructions

1. Begin by washing and drying each piece of food. If you're not using organic foods, soak them to remove pesticides. To do this, soak fruits and vegetables in a sink filled with ½ cup baking soda and a bit of dish soap. Let them soak for 20 minutes. Then drain, rinse in cool water, and dry well.

2. Pre-treat any foods that require it. Some foods may need to be blanched, boiled, or dipped.

3. Blanching involves heating food in steam or water and then cooling quickly in an ice bath.

4. Boiling is required to soften certain foods before dehydrating.

5. Dipping involves treating food with citric acid or lemon juice to prevent oxidation.

6. Preheat the dehydrator. Most fruits and vegetables will dry at 135ºF, but confirm this for each item before doing so.

7. Place food in single layers on trays. Foods that may become sticky should not touch at all. Use parchment paper liners for sticky foods.

8. Always keep five trays in the dehydrator for circulation reasons. Check your food halfway through.

9. Vegetables are ready when they're brittle, and fruits are ready once they doesn't release any juice when squeezed.

REHYDRATING

Rehydrating dried foods allows you to use them as if they were fresh. While each food may have its own particular needs for rehydration, there are a few guidelines that will serve you well more often than not. To rehydrate fruits, cover them with boiling water and let them soak for 10 minutes. Then drain and use immediately.

Vegetables are similar. You'll add an equal ratio of vegetables and boiling water, and let them sit for between 15 minutes and three hours, depending on the food. When it's ready, use it immediately.

Having a stash of dehydrated food is a great way for you to add some variety to your diet and have easily portable snacks as well. Many foods can be dehydrated well, and while it's not recommended for you to dehydrate dairy products, you can still enjoy many dried foods. Fruits can be mixed into oatmeal. Vegetables can be used to enrich sauces. Meats can be enjoyed as jerky. With dehydration as easy as it is, there's no reason to skip it.

Chapter Summary

In this chapter, we discussed how to dehydrate and rehydrate foods.

- Dehydration removes moisture so food doesn't go moldy.
- Certain foods must be blanched, boiled, dipped, or cooked before they can be dehydrated.

- In a pinch, food can be dehydrated in the sun or the oven, but the most consistent way to do it is with a designated dehydrator.
- Rehydration is as simple as soaking foods in boiling water for prescribed amounts of time.

9

PRESERVING AND PICKLING: INTRODUCING THE FORGOTTEN ART YOUR GRANDPARENTS KNEW ALL ABOUT

I f you have a bounty of fresh berries or fruits that you need to preserve, you can do so with preserves. Likewise, a glut of cabbage or cucumbers could become a bounty of pickled foods that are tasty, healthy, and fun to snack on. Our grandparents once used these arts to protect and preserve their harvests for long after the growing season. Jams and jellies can retain up to 70% of the nutritional value of fruits, and they taste great. However, they are loaded with sugar, and you typically only eat a small amount at a time. Pickling is much more nutritionally balanced, especially if you choose methods that will ferment the foods. However, be mindful of a high salt content, as this could be detrimental to the effect you're trying to create.

THE BENEFITS OF PICKLING

Pickling offers several benefits that make it a worthwhile skill to learn in order to fill your pantry. These include:

- **Food preservation:** When you pickle food, you extend its shelf-life, especially if you don't have access to refrigerators. Pickled foods are soaked in vinegar or something of high acidity to prevent spoilage.
- **Reduced food storage cost:** While freezing is currently the most commonly used long-term storage solution for food, it is also expensive

when compared to other options. Pickled food remains stable at room temperature.

- **Flavor:** Pickling was originally done to preserve food, but it also allows food to taste much better. Corned beef, for example, is pickled. Sauerkraut on a hot dog? Pickled. Kimchi? Pickled. Pickled foods are often delicious and worth the effort you put into preparing them.
- **Health benefits:** Pickled foods, especially when they're fermented, are substantial sources of nutrients. The sodium content in the brine can also relieve muscle cramps after sweating, and boost hydration when consumed in moderation.

PICKLING METHODS

Pickling is the process of using some sort of high-acid solution (typically either vinegar or a fermented substance) to preserve food. When the environment is high in acidity, the food cannot go bad. A high acidity environment can be created through salt or vinegar.

Pickling follows just a few key steps: brining, packing in jars, covering with hot vinegar, and usually processing in a water bath. Pickled foods can then be stored somewhere cool and dark. Most often, they should be left to sit for eight weeks to develop flavor, but no one's judging if you crack into them sooner!

Pickling with Salt

Pickling with salt can be done either with dry salt or with brine. When using the dry salt method, you combine dry salt with vegetables. As the vegetables sit, the liquid is pulled out of them and creates the brine. Other times, a pre-made brine can be mixed into the vegetables to soak for a set amount of time. In this state, vegetables will ferment, which is the process during which bacteria in foods converts the sugar into lactic acid, which is a natural preservative. This is the most common method of preserving foods that usually don't process and preserve well, like cabbage, which can become kimchi or sauerkraut. Pickled foods will last for up to a year.

Pickling with Vinegar

Typically, using vinegar is a much quicker process because there's no fermentation of the vegetables. They will sit in brine for a while, which aids the flavor and crispness, before being drained, boiled in vinegar, packed in jars with more vinegar, and then water bath-canned to seal the jars. Vinegar has acetic acid, which boosts acidity and prevents microorganisms from developing.

When pickling foods, you must use very fresh ingredients or you will end up with mushy results. If you're planning on making a batch of pickled vegetables, try to pickle them as soon as they've been picked. You want to catch the food at peak freshness.

When pickling, you'll only need salt or vinegar and water. You can use both in some situations. When using salt, ensure that it is always pickling or kosher salt. These salts are free from anti-caking agents that could cause cloudiness. This isn't harmful, but it will affect the appearance. You can add other ingredients as well. Often, sugar, herbs, spices, and garlic can be added to create different varieties of flavors.

Some people choose to use firming agents for crisping up vegetables. They often turn to lime or alum. Lime is calcium hydroxide, and alum is potassium aluminum phosphate. These aren't necessary, but can be used, and you may see them in recipes from time to time.

PICKLE RECIPES

If you're interested in pickling, it's a good idea to get a recipe book to provide you with a variety of options. You can experiment with many flavor profiles, which is often welcome if you have a glut of a single vegetable.

We'll go over three recipes here, but many, many others could be used.

Pickled Garlic

Pickled garlic is a great way to use up a glut of garlic. It's flavorful, and mellows out the bite garlic has while accentuating the flavor. It prolongs its shelf-life while balancing the flavors. This recipe yields 1 quart.

Ingredients

- Bay leaf (1, sliced in half)
- Cumin seeds (⅛ tsp)
- Coriander seeds (⅛ tsp)
- Crushed red chili peppers (¼ tsp, reduce if you prefer less spice)
- Peppercorns (¼ tsp)
- White wine vinegar (1¼ cup)
- Mustard seeds (⅛ tsp)
- Kosher salt (1 Tbsp)
- Garlic (4 cups, peeled)

Equipment

- Pint-sized mason jars
- Saucepan
- Spoon

Instructions

1. Wash both jars and lids in boiling water to sterilize them, then set them aside.
2. Combine vinegar, 1 cup of water, and salt in a saucepan and bring to the boil, then reduce to a low heat and cover.
3. At the bottom of each jar, layer equal amounts of each spice: peppercorns, cumin, coriander, red chili pepper, mustard seeds, and bay leaf.
4. Pack each jar with as much garlic as possible, leaving ½ inch free at the top.
5. Pour in the salt and vinegar mixture, leaving a ¼-inch headspace. Push down the garlic, and make sure bubbles are released. Clean the rims and screw on the lids.
6. Pickle it in the refrigerator for three days, or use standard canning procedures to seal the jars.

Pickled Kimchi

Kimchi can be made simply using a handful of good ingredients. This recipe will yield several quart-sized jars, depending on how tightly you choose to pack the jars. Keep extra jars on hand, just in case.

Ingredients

- Green cabbage (1 head, cut into 1"x2" pieces with a few leaves uncut)
- Kosher salt (2 Tbsp)
- Garlic (2–3 large cloves, minced)
- Ginger (1 tsp, peeled and grated)
- Sugar (1 tsp)
- Gochugaru, Korean chili pepper (3 Tbsp)
- Green onions (4, green parts only)
- Onion (1 medium, sliced thinly)

Equipment

- Quart-sized mason jars (sterilized)
- Large bowl
- Knife and cutting board
- Wooden spoon
- Blender

Instructions

1. Begin by washing and pre-measuring all ingredients so they're ready to go.
2. Put the cabbage into a large bowl, reserving a few large leaves. Sprinkle it with salt and mix to combine. Cover the bowl and let the

contents sit until wilted (between 1 and 12 hours).

3. Combine the garlic, ginger, onion, green onion, sugar, and chili pepper in the blender. Process to create a rough paste. Then check the cabbage.

4. When the cabbage is ready, drain it, reserving the liquid, and pat the leaves dry.

5. Combine the cabbage with the spice paste, mixing well.

6. Push the kimchi into jars as tightly as possible. Add liquid to each jar, leaving at least 1 inch of headspace. Water can be added if you run out of liquid to completely cover the kimchi. Push the mixture down.

7. Cover the top of each jar with one cabbage leaf. Loosely seal the jars and let them sit at room temperature for between three and five days, tasting regularly. It's done when it's sour and spicy.

8. When it's ready, remove the cabbage leaves from the top and store the jars in the fridge, tightly sealed.

Pickled Sauerkraut

Sauerkraut is created when lactobacillus, beneficial bacteria on the surface of food, ferments. This occurs when food is dipped into a brine, where the bacteria can start converting sugars into lactic acid which preserves the food. In this case, sauerkraut results from cabbage fermenting, at around 55ºF, for several months. If you don't have a cellar or a cool garage, you could also store it in your fridge. The benefit is that, after the fermentation process, there will be plenty of healthy probiotics included in it.

Ingredients

- 1 head of green cabbage (roughly 3 lb)
- Kosher salt (1.5 Tbsp)
- Caraway seeds (optional, but they add flavor)

Equipment

- Canning funnel
- 2-quart canning jar (or two 1-quart mason jars)
- Mixing bowl
- Jelly jar to fit into the canning jar (or 2 if using mason jars)
- Stones, marbles, or weights to weigh down the jelly jar
- Cheesecloth
- Rubber band

Instructions

1. Begin by cleaning all your equipment. Ensure the jars are sanitized, and then wash your hands well.
2. Remove any wilted leaves around the cabbage, and cut it into quarters, trimming the core and discarding it. Then create eight wedges. Each wedge should then be sliced into thin ribbons, reminiscent of sauerkraut.
3. Put the cabbage in a bowl, and sprinkle it with salt. Use your hands to massage and squeeze the cabbage to spread the salt around. Do so for 5–10 minutes to get a consistency reminiscent of coleslaw. Then add in the caraway seeds if you're using them.
4. Pack handfuls of the cabbage into the canning jar using the funnel. Make sure you push down the cabbage from time to time to keep it packed in there.
5. Slide the jelly jar into the mouth of the canning jar, weighing it down with stones or marbles. This will keep all the cabbage weighed down and submerged in its liquid.
6. Cover the jar with cheesecloth, then secure it with a rubber band. This protects the

sauerkraut from dust and insects, while also allowing for airflow.

7. Push down the cabbage every few hours for the next 24 hours to release more liquid.

8. After 24 hours, you can add more brine if the liquid does not cover the cabbage. To do so, dissolve 1 tsp of salt in a cup of water, and pour in just enough to completely cover the cabbage.

9. Let the cabbage ferment out of sunlight and in a cool room for three to 10 days. Taste it from Day 3. When you've achieved the desired taste, you can then refrigerate it. If it begins to develop mold, skim off the moldy part and ensure the rest of the cabbage is submerged.

Chapter Summary

In this chapter, we reviewed the process of pickling to preserve foods. Key points to remember are:

- Jams and jellies preserve a lot of nutritional value, but are not very effective as they are eaten in small quantities.
- Pickling alters the flavor of a food, but is a great way to preserve its health benefits.
- Pickling can be done with salt, brine, or vinegar. When using salt or brine, fermentation

occurs. When using vinegar, there is no fermentation.

10

EMERGENCY BACK UP: A NOTE ON VITAMINS AND SUPPLEMENTS

While your regular diet should be enough to provide you with all the nutritional benefits you need, it's always good to be prepared in case you can't eat as you normally would. Having vitamins and supplements means that even if you lose food, you can still keep up with the nutritional requirements of your body.

Buying vitamins isn't as straightforward as just picking up the cheapest option on the shelf, however, and you'll get what you pay for. This means that you want to buy the best, highest quality vitamins you can because cheaper options usually use subpar ingredients that may not be as easy for your body to absorb.

As you read through this chapter, we are going to address several important topics related to vitamins and supplements. First, we will discuss the best vitamins to keep and store. Then we'll address the shelf-life of various vitamins. Finally, we'll discuss which vitamins and minerals you should prioritize.

Selecting Vitamins

Consider the various age groups that are part of your family. For example, if you have young children, make sure you have vitamins designed for younger children, as some vitamins can be overdosed on when consumed in the wrong quantities. If you have a pregnant or lactating woman in the house, have some vitamin supplements targeted to her. Women of childbearing age must have folate in higher quantities to prevent early birth defects that may occur before a woman even knows she's pregnant. Even if there are no plans to become pregnant, it may be a good idea to keep some prenatal-specific vitamins on hand, as life sometimes has its own ideas.

A complete one-a-day vitamin is usually the easiest option for each group, but you can buy vitamins individually as well. The easiest option would be to have children's one-a-day vitamins, adult vitamins, prenatal vitamins (if applicable), and senior vitamins, especially if you or anyone in your home is aging. When selecting vitamins, opt for those that are food-based. These will be most of the organic vitamins you find. However, if you can't, any vitamins are better than none.

Age-based vitamins are a significant consideration, as are sex-based ones, as people at different life stages will have different needs. In a pinch, a child should be able to take adult vitamins, but ONLY if there is no iron included. Children can get sick from iron if they get too much of it.

When selecting the type of vitamin to get, you'll notice that there are several options. You can get gummies or gels, which may be easier to take, but may not last as long as tablet or powder forms. You need to weigh longevity against taste, and in a survival or emergency situation, most people will opt for longevity over anything else.

What Is the Shelf-Life of Vitamin Supplements?

Vitamins and minerals can be stored for a sufficient period. Some may be good for up to 15 years, depending on storage, conditions, and the quality of the vitamins. If you store vitamins in a garage, where they're exposed to constantly fluctuating temperatures, they may not last nearly as long. Those stored in a pantry or a refrigerator may last longer. However, they will gradually decrease in potency as they age.

The use-by date on the vitamin packages is a suggestion. It is the point until which the potency of the vitamin stops being guaranteed. However, they may last longer than this. You can judge the shelf-life based on:

- The Vitamin: Some are more sensitive than others. Vitamin A is sensitive to light. Folic acid is stable in oxygen, but sensitive to heat and light. B12 is stable.
- Binders Added: Some binders may interact with the vitamins, which could affect the shelf-life. Ascorbic acid, for example, is reactive because of being an acid. Most vitamins are acidic, and therefore reactive.

Shelf-life calculations are conservative. Even though your vitamins will lose potency over time, they still can provide you with plenty of benefits. To store them, keep them in their original packaging in cool, dry conditions. Make sure they are somewhere away from light, heat, oxygen, and humidity. A good idea is to place them inside a box or a light-proof container, and then place them somewhere cool. This provides several layers of protection against deterioration.

Keep in mind that while it's best to consume vitamins and supplements when recommended by the manufacturer, vitamin supplements do not go bad in the sense that they will become harmful. They will lose potency, but they will not become dangerous to your health. As long as they do not smell or look off, they should be fine.

What Vitamins Do I Need to Stock Up On?

Vitamins C and D should be prioritized for immune health, but it's good to store several others too. If possible, buy in bulk with larger bottles so you have plenty available. However, remember that just like with food, vitamins will deteriorate when exposed to heat, light, or humidity, so storage in cool, dry packages is essential. If you can keep them in a cold location, they'll remain in good condition for longer.

You want to choose pure forms in tablet or powder form to keep the vitamins at their best for as long as possible. Gelcaps have oils which will go rancid, and gummies will go bad because of moisture. Keep in mind that supplements with live bacteria (probiotics) are unlikely to keep very long, as the bacteria will die off. However, kimchi and sauerkraut, or other fermented foods, offer similar benefits to probiotic tablets.

The vitamins that are the weakest are vitamin B12 and vitamin C. For vitamin C, you could use L-ascorbic acid powder, which will remain stable for longer. One good way to store vitamins is to use a good multivitamin tablet, along with the ascorbic acid powder.

Vitamins and minerals are essential to your health, and without them, you won't feel well. In an emergency, where time is of the essence and you may need to hunt, work the land, or protect yourself, you can't risk suffering from malnutrition that can leave you ineffective. Having a stockpile of good multivitamins can help to ensure that even when food is scarce, you are nourished enough to maintain your health.

Chapter Summary

In this chapter, we reviewed the importance of supplementation and vitamins as a backup in case there is anything that prevents you from accessing a healthy diet.

- Multivitamins are the easiest way to cover all bases.
- Keep age- and sex-specific vitamins on hand according to your family's needs. Children and adults have different vitamin needs.
- In a pinch, a child can take adult vitamins that do not contain iron.
- Women of childbearing age must get enough folate to prevent birth defects should they get

pregnant, so if there is a woman in the house, ensure that she has a folate-rich supplement.

- Store vitamins and minerals in a cool, dark, dry spot in their original packaging.
- The shelf life of vitamins is a conservative recommendation, and many tablets will be good for 10–15 years if stored properly.
- Vitamins B12 and C are the most fragile.
- Store vitamin C as L-ascorbic acid powder, as it is nonreactive in this form.

NOW FOR THE BEST PART!

You get to help our community by giving this book a review.

Many preppers, just like you, know how hard it is to find current, concise, and useful information, especially when starting. Not only will your review help them on their prepping journey, but the information you direct them to might also save their lives!

Do another prepper a favor and leave a review talking about the information you found, what you liked about the book, and how it helped you... even if it just a sentence or two!

Customer Reviews

⭐⭐⭐⭐⭐ 2
5.0 out of 5 stars ▾

5 star		100%
4 star		0%
3 star		0%
2 star		0%
1 star		0%

See all verified purchase reviews ›

Share your thoughts with other customers

Write a customer review ⬅

I am so very appreciative of your review, as it truly makes a difference in our community.

Thank you from the bottom of my heart for purchasing this book. I hope our paths cross again in the future.

Scan this QR code and leave a brief review on Amazon.

CONCLUSION

No one knows when disaster will strike. No one can predict when roads may be blocked, food shortages may prevent access to healthy foods, or war or catastrophic emergency may end life as we know it. We've already seen this relatively recently with the COVID-19 pandemic. No one expected that there would be something that could shut down the entire world. Yet restrictions around the world have caused shortages of many foods we once took for granted. Who's to say that next time won't be worse?

The COVID-19 pandemic was a major eye-opener for many people who never thought that anything bad could happen to them in their suburban, middle-class home, yet disaster happened. Flour and sugar were off the shelves for a while. Bread and pasta? Good luck.

While shopping has returned to normal in most places, there are still echoes of shortages, and uncertainty remains: What if it happens again? Will you be prepared? Will you know what you need to keep stashed to ensure that your family will eat, no matter what happens?

Reading this book was the perfect first step to assuaging those fears, and now you've done so, you can start taking action. You've learnt everything you need to know to set up your very own food storage to prevent your family from suffering from malnutrition should anything prevent you from accessing resources normally. We live in strange and uncertain times, so being prepared is more important than ever. If you can't access food, it's your health and the health of your family that are most at risk.

Your family relies on you to ensure that they have everything they need. Your children look to you to make sure there is always food on the table. Perhaps you have a partner who relies on you too. Preparation can help you navigate difficult times and last long enough for help to arrive, or until you can start working toward self-sufficiency in other ways.

As you read through this book, you were guided through several key points to help you prepare in case another crisis hits suburbia. We went over the essentials of maintaining a healthy body, as well as the nutrients your body needs. We discussed how to keep your immune system in peak condition with the foods you choose. From there, we discussed several game plans to stock up your pantry with confidence. From shopping trips to stock up the pantry to gardening your way towards self-sufficiency, we explored ways to ensure that food will be available if disaster strikes.

We also discussed several storage options to help you keep your food for as long as possible. We discussed the best methods for dry storage in the pantry to keep your food from rotting, from being infested with insects or rodents, and from losing flavor. We discussed how to can to maintain nutrition, and how to do so safely to prevent botulism. We went over stocking a chest freezer and how to keep it functioning for as long as possible. We addressed dehydration as an alternate method to store foods long-term. We went over how to pickle vegetables that may otherwise not preserve well. And finally, we discussed a game plan for stocking up on vitamins that will ensure that no matter what the situation, you and your family will have essential nutrients.

You have all the tools at your disposal at this point. You know what you need, how you can get it, and how it can all be kept and stored to ensure that it's there when you need it. What happens from here is up to you. Aim for a stockpile of food to last you and your family three to six months, by which time, you should be able to stabilize and find alternative sources of food if necessary. You owe it to yourself to be prepared, and now you are.

Thank you for taking the time to read through this book as your introduction to creating your very own stockpile of food. Hopefully, as you read, you found plenty of information that was useful to you. Hopefully, you feel a bit more at ease that even if disaster strikes, you can still get by if you know what you're doing. You've got the knowledge. You can learn the skills. And then you'll survive.

If you feel more confident, please consider leaving your thoughts and feelings in a review to spread the word and help others prepare as well.

The human species is incredibly adaptable. It's versatile. It can survive in just about any environment. You can do this too if you put your mind to it. You already have the mindset of prepping. Now it's about implementation.

T.Riley

Would your family survive in lockdown if society were to collapse? Learn how to prepare your home now.

We are used to a world in which our homes are supplied with fresh water, gas, and electricity.

We're used to having our waste removed and our sanitary needs met.

These are all things we've come to expect, but what would happen if they were taken away?

Flooding, hurricanes, and pandemics are affecting areas we once thought were safe from disaster--we shouldn't take anything for granted.

In When Crisis Hits Suburbia: A Modern-Day Prepping Guide to Effectively Bug In and Protect Your Family Home in a Societal Collapse, you'll learn exactly what you need to know to prepare your home for an emergency. You'll find:

- The 6 key priorities of survival and how to make sure you have them covered
- A clear guide for knowing when it's time to stay in, and when it's time to evacuate
- Top prepper survival secrets so that you always stay one step ahead of the rest
- A toolbox of information that allows you to choose what works best for your family
- Practical tips for preparing your children for worst-case scenarios without frightening them
- How to make sure your water supply is 100% safe at all times
- Comprehensive checklists for everything you need to stock in your home
- Essential administrative tasks you should have sorted in advance before a disaster strikes

And much more.

The ideal home is not only the home that keeps you and your family safe in good times, but it's the home that keeps you safe no matter what.

Prepare your home for the worst-case scenario and protect your family no matter what.

A Special Gift to My Readers

Included with your purchase of this book is your free
copy of the *Emergency Information Planner*

Follow the link below to receive your copy:
www.tedrileyauthor.com
Or by accessing the QR code:

You can also join our Facebook community **Suburban
Prepping with Ted**, or contact me directly via
ted@tedrileyauthor.com.

REFERENCES

Bellew, P. (2016, March 21). *33 Essential Foods to Stock Pile*. Ask a Prepper. https://www.askaprepper.com/33-essential-foods-to-stock-pile/

Better Health Channel. (n.d.). *Immune System Explained*. https://www.betterhealth.vic.gov.au/health/conditionsandtreatments/immune-system

Biggers, S. (2021, May 24). *The Best Vitamins and Supplements for Hard Times*. Backdoor Survival. https://www.backdoorsurvival.com/the-best-vitamins-and-supplements-for-hard-times/

Bone, E. (2013, December 13). *Food Preservation Techniques: Learn How to Pickle*. The Prepper Journal. https://www.theprepperjournal.com/2013/10/11/food-preservation-techniques-learn-pickle/

Bradford, A. (2018, July 26). *Upright Freezer or Chest Freezer: Which Should You Buy?* CNET. https://www.cnet.com/how-to/upright-freezer-vs-chest-freezer/

Brown, C. (2020, January 9). *Common Home Preservation Methods: Advantages and Disadvantages.* Delishably. https://delishably.com/sauces-preserves/homepreservationadvantagesanddisadvantagespt2

Burgess, L. (2018, July 10). *The Best Foods for Boosting Your Immune System.* Medical News Today. https://www.medicalnewstoday.com/articles/322412#which-foods-boost-the-immune-system

Carter, B. (n.d.). *DIY Dehydrated-Foods Guide.* US Preppers. https://uspreppers.com/diy-dehydrated-foods-guide/

Childs, C., Calder, P., & Miles, E. (2019, August 16). Diet and Immune Function. *Nutrients, 11(8), 1933.* https://doi.org/10.3390/nu11081933

Christensen, E. (2020, January 29). *How to Make Home-made Sauerkraut in a Mason Jar.* Kitchn. https://www.thekitchn.com/how-to-make-homemade-sauerkraut-in-a-mason-jar-193124

Clay, J. (1992, August/September). *Home Canning for Beginners: How to Can Your Food Year-Round.* Mother

Earth News. https://www.motherearthnews.com/real-food/home-canning-for-beginners-zmaz92aszshe

David, N. (2018, February 28). *Frozen Food Storage.* PreppersSurvive. http://www.prepperssurvive.com/frozen-food-storage/

Grey, S. (2019, January 10). *The Advantages of Pickling Foods.* Our Everyday Life. https://oureverydaylife.com/548285-the-advantages-of-pickling-foods.html

Gunnars, K. (2018, September 5). *10 Surprising Health Benefits of Honey.* Healthline. https://www.healthline.com/nutrition/10-benefits-of-honey#section10

Gunnars, K. (2021, April 8). *6 Health Benefits of Apple Cider Vinegar, Backed by Science.* Healthline. https://www.healthline.com/nutrition/6-proven-health-benefits-of-apple-cider-vinegar

Hanus, R. (2013, December 12). *The 5 Minute Prepper #15: Make Freezing Part of Your Food Storage.* The Grow Network. https://thegrownetwork.com/the-5-minute-prepper-15-make-freezing-part-of-your-food-storage/

HappyPreppers.com. (n.d.). *How to Dehydrate Foods.* https://www.happypreppers.com/Dehydrating.html

HappyPreppers.com. (n.d.). *Super Immunity Boosters.* https://www.happypreppers.com/immunity.html

Harvard Health Publishing. (2021, February 15) *How to Boost Your Immune System*. https://www.health.harvard.edu/staying-healthy/how-to-boost-your-immune-system

Healthy Canning. (2020, July 19). *Canning Vegetables*. https://www.healthycanning.com/canning-vegetables/

Henry, P. (2013, February 16). *Prepping 101—Prepper Food Storage*. The Prepper Journal. https://www.theprepperjournal.com/2013/02/16/prepper-101-food-preps-30-days-worth-of-food/

Higgs, J. (2019, July 15). *How to Store Food for Long Term Storage in Case of Emergency*. Caltex Plastics. https://caltexplastics.com/store-food-longterm.html

Jones, K. (2019, December 17). *Shelf-Life of Vitamin Supplements in a Survival Food Supply*. The Provident Prepper. https://theprovidentprepper.org/shelf-life-of-vitamin-supplements-in-a-survival-food-supply/

Jones, K. (2021, February 04). *Long Term Food Storage: Best Containers and Treatment Methods*. The Provident Prepper. https://theprovidentprepper.org/long-term-food-storage-best-containers-and-treatment-methods/

Jorgustin, K. (2018, December 14). *Survival Vitamins and Supplements*. Modern Survival Blog. https://

modernsurvivalblog.com/preps/survival-prep-vitamins-and-medications/

Just in Case Jack. (2016, July 19). *Emergency Food Storage: How to Build Your Survival Food System.* Skilled Survival. https://www.skilledsurvival.com/emergency-food-supply-how-to-get-started/

Kubala, J (2021, June 24). *The Definitive Guide to Healthy Eating in Real Life.* Healthline. https://www.healthline.com/nutrition/how-to-eat-healthy-guide

Lehman, S. (2021, February 08). *The Basics of a Healthy, Balanced Diet.* Verywell Fit. https://www.verywellfit.com/the-basics-of-a-healthy-balanced-diet-2506675

Matheny, M. (2016, August 20). *Easy Pickled Garlic: For Refrigerating or Canning.* The Yummy Life. https://www.theyummylife.com/Pickled_Garlic

McClellan, M. (2019, October 10). *A Beginner's Guide to Canning.* Serious Eats. https://www.seriouseats.com/2012/02/how-to-can-canning-pickling-preserving-ball-jars-materials-siphoning-recipes.html

McIntosh, J. (2019, October 9). *Everything You Need to Know about Eggs.* Medical News Today. https://www.medicalnewstoday.com/articles/283659

McMordie, K. (2018, August 29). *Beginner's Guide to Canning.* Lively Table. https://livelytable.com/beginners-guide-to-canning/

Mitchell, C. (n.d.). *Experts Explain Which Foods You Should Stockpile before Dealing with a Natural Disaster.* AccuWeather. https://www.accuweather.com/en/weather-news/experts-explain-which-foods-you-should-stockpile-before-dealing-with-a-natural-disaster-2/432899

Newcomer, L. (2013, May 21). *Hot and Healthy: How to Make Better Kimchi at Home.* Greatist. https://greatist.com/health/how-to-make-your-own-diy-kimchi

Nick, J. (2021, February 18). *7 Ways You Can Make Your Garlic Last Longer.* Good Housekeeping. https://www.goodhousekeeping.com/food-recipes/a20707233/how-to-store-garlic/

Pierce, R. (2019, August 15). *The Ultimate List of What You Can (and Cannot!) Can.* J&R Pierce Family Farm. https://jrpiercefamilyfarm.com/2019/08/15/the-ultimate-list-of-what-you-can-and-cannot-can/

Powitz, R. (2005, June 1). *7 Simple Rules for Effective and Hygienic Dry Goods Storage.* Food Safety Magazine. https://www.foodsafetymagazine.com/magazine-archive1/junejuly-2005/7-simple-rules-for-effective-and-hygienic-dry-goods-storage/

Ready. (n.d.). *Food.* https://www.ready.gov/food

RecipeTips. (n.d.). *Canning Temperatures and Processing Times.* https://www.recipetips.com/kitchen-tips/t--1396/canning-temperatures-and-processing-times.asp

Russell, P. (2016, December 6). *A Beginner's Guide to Canning at Home.* Instructables. https://www.instructables.com/A-Beginners-Guide-to-Canning-at-Home/

Schend, J. (2020, April 30). *15 Foods That Boost the Immune System.* Healthline. https://www.healthline.com/health/food-nutrition/foods-that-boost-the-immune-system

Science Daily. (2019, September 04). *Many Older Adults Aren't Fully Prepared for Emergency Situations, Poll Finds.* https://www.sciencedaily.com/releases/2019/09/190904081313.htm

Spurr, T. (2015, October 14). *Blackberry Jam. Full of Goodness or a "Devil's Food"?* Eat Yourself Brilliant. http://www.eatyourselfbrilliant.co.uk/blackberry-jam-full-of-goodness-or-a-devils-food/

Stone, K. (2018, November 27). *How to Dehydrate Food for Beginners.* Stone Family Farmstead. https://stonefamilyfarmstead.com/how-to-dehydrate-food/

Szalay, J. (2015, December 10). *What Is Protein?* Live Science. https://www.livescience.com/53044-protein.html

Szalay, J. (2015, December 18). *What Is Dietary Fat?* Live Science. https://www.livescience.com/53145-dietary-fat.html

Szalay, J. (2017, July 14). *What Are Carbohydrates?* Live Science. https://www.livescience.com/51976-carbohydrates.html

U.S. Food and Drug Administration (n.d.). *Nutrition Facts Labeling Requirements.* https://www.fda.gov/media/99069/download

Printed in Great Britain
by Amazon

74289470R00123